IRAQ

AN ILLUSTRATED
HISTORY AND GUIDE

by Gilles Munier

photography by Erick Bonnier
translated by David Stryker

Interlink Books

An imprint of Interlink Publishing Group, Inc.
Northampton, Massachusetts

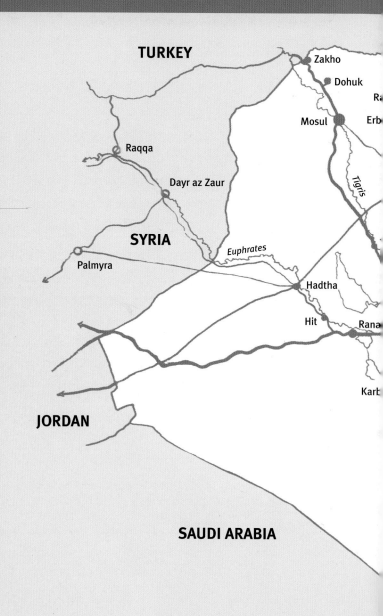

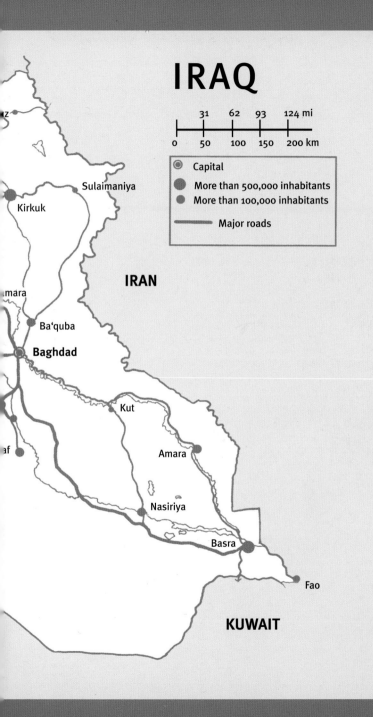

IRAQ

31   62   93   124 mi

0   50   100   150   200 km

- ◉ Capital
- ● More than 500,000 inhabitants
- ● More than 100,000 inhabitants
- —— Major roads

z

Sulaimaniya

Kirkuk

IRAN

mara

Ba'quba

Baghdad

Kut

Amara

af

Nasiriya

Basra

Fao

KUWAIT

First American edition published 2004 by

INTERLINK BOOKS
An imprint of Interlink Publishing Group, Inc.
46 Crosby Street, Northampton, Massachusetts 01060
www.interlinkbooks.com

Copyright © by Gilles Munier 2000, 2004
Photography © Erick Bonnier 2000, 2004 unless otherwise noted in the text
English translation © Interlink Publishing Group, Inc. 2004
Some photographs are from the personal collection of the author
Maps by Nelson Martinez
Calligraphy by Ghani Alani

Originally published in French as *Guide de l'Irak,* les Guides Picollec

Library of Congress Cataloging-in-Publication Data
Munier, Gilles.
[Guide de l'Irak. English]
Iraq : an illustrated history / by Gilles Munier. — 1st American ed.
p. cm.
Includes bibliographical references.
ISBN 1-56656-513-8 (pbk.)
1. Iraq—History. 2. Iraq—Guidebooks. I. Title.
DS70.9.M8613 2003
956.7—dc21

2003013372

Printed and bound in Korea

To request our complete 40-page full-color catalog,
please call us toll free at **1-800-238-LINK,** visit our website at **www.interlinkbooks.com,**
or write to **Interlink Publishing** • 46 Crosby Street • Northampton, MA • 01060
e-mail: sales@interlinkbooks.com

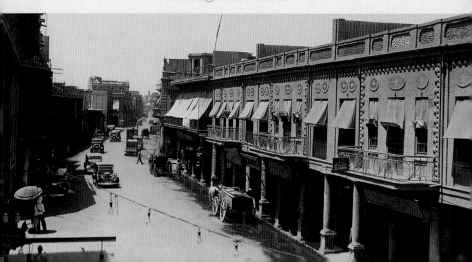

Publisher's Note

While public opinion around the world did not see an imminent threat to the security of the United States or Great Britain, the invasion of Iraq began in March 2003, with disastrous consequences. In what President Bush called "one of the swiftest and most humane military campaigns in history," thousands of Iraqi lives perished, hundreds of US and British service people were killed, Iraq's infrastructure was largely devastated, its museums and archaeological treasures were looted, and "tens of billions" (in the words of L. Paul Bremer III, the chief American administrator of Iraq) in facilities essential to survival were destroyed, which left the whole country destitute and literally burning with rage and uncontrolled violence.

All this, we were told, was done in the name of a noble cause: that of democracy, freedom, and "liberating" the Iraqi people. But, apart from the knowledge that Iraq had vast oil reserves, how much did we really know about the people of Iraq, their history, their culture, their aspirations?

During and after the build-up to war, publishers and editors the world over were scrambling to put together "instant" books on Iraq. So-called "experts" were born overnight and Iraq-related books—on subjects ranging from weapons of mass destructions, to sanctions, to military strategy, to personal accounts of heroism—filled the shelves in bookstores. But despite the abundance of "Iraq" books, hardly any gave readers a clear insight into Iraq's rich history or contributed to a better understanding of the Iraqi people and their culture.

We were actively looking for an author to write a concise, yet comprehensive, overview of Iraq when this beautifully illustrated historical guidebook—originally published in France just before the war—came across our desks. "Isn't it a bad idea," someone asked, "to publish a book from France at a time when many folks are pouring French wine down their toilets to protest France's anti-war stance?" "Don't you think it is foolish," someone else said, "to publish an historical guidebook in time of war?" Our reply is: absolutely not— there is no better time. We felt, how important at this point in time to bring out a book whose entire *raison d'etre* is to assume that Iraq is a country anyone might want to visit: for the beauty of its landscape and architecture, for its central role in thousands of years in human history, for the warmth and hospitality its people are so renowned for. Who wouldn't want to see some of the most ancient archeological sites in the world? Sip tea in a café that's been around since the Ottomans? Feel the breeze stirring the branches of Adam and Eve's tree?

As this book goes to press, the removal of the notoriously repressive government of Saddam Hussein has been replaced by an absence of administration and law and order. In short, Iraq is a mess, the tempo of attacks against the occupation forces has intensified, the post-war death toll of American and British soldiers has exceeded the wartime total, and the world resents America and Great Britain for their defiance of the international community.

How long will the occupation last, and what will it bring to the people of Iraq? It is hard to say. But we can say: consider what wisdom history holds; consider what it's like being Iraqi. Read. Learn. Imagine.

Aerial view of Baghdad in the 1920s.

— ONE —

Introduction

Until World War I, Iraq was known in the Western world as Mesopotamia, cradle of ancient civilizations. But Arabs had used the name Iraq, which was formally adopted in 1921, since the Middle Ages. The caliphs of the Abbasid dynasty a thousand years ago designated the region of the Tigris and Euphrates rivers by the term al-Iraq al-Arabi; northwestern Persia was called al-Iraq al-Ajami. An ancient Aramaic word, Iraq means "black, muddy land."

Geography

Iraq occupies a total area of about 168,000 square miles (about 438,000 km²), which makes it slightly larger than California. The Tigris and the Euphrates, two great rivers that have played major roles in the region's history, run through the country, flowing southeast toward the Gulf. Thanks to these rivers and their tributaries—the Greater Zab, the Lesser Zab, and the Diyala—Iraq possesses vast hydraulic resources and highly arable land, irrigated by numerous canals. The Tigris and the Euphrates join just north of Basra, and the resulting Shatt al-Arab ("River of the Arabs") empties into the Gulf along the border with Iran.

In ancient times, this narrow body of water between the Arabian Peninsula and the western coast of Iran was called, among other names, the Sea of the Rising Sun. Its most common name was the Chaldean Sea. When the Persians occupied Mesopotamia in 539 BCE, it became the Persian Gulf. But there has long been an overwhelming presence of Arab populations on both sides of the Gulf, even on the Iranian (or Persian) side, at least in the southwestern coastal region of Khuzistan, which borders Iraq. Soon after World War I, the British dashed the

ambitions of Shaykh Khazal, ruler of this province, by naming Faisal I to
the throne of Iraq. But even today, if local independence movements
had their way, Khuzistan might still be referred to as Arabistan. So one
can understand why, for Arab peoples, the Gulf is Arab, not Persian.
And for that matter, why for Iranians it is the Persian Gulf. The war of
the 1980s between the two countries is only the most recent in a long
series of conflicts between two ancient civilizations, and the names and
borders throughout the region tell the history of this and other
conquests and reconquests.

Iraq borders Saudi Arabia, Jordan, and Syria to the west, Iran to the
east, and Turkey to the north. These frontiers are the result of a largely
artificial plan implemented by the British and the French after World
War I, and have given rise to periodic conflicts, in particular with Iran
and Kuwait, and with the Kurds.

Iraq is administratively divided into 18 provinces, three of which
make up the Kurdistan Autonomous Region. Baghdad, the capital, is
situated in the center of the country. The other major cities of Iraq are
Mosul, Basra, Kirkuk, Hilla, Karbala and Najaf (holy cities of the Shi'a
Muslims), Tikrit (birthplace of the famous leader, Saladin, and Saddam
Hussein), and Erbil (capital of Kurdistan).

The southwest of the country, near the Jordanian and Saudi Arabian
borders, is a rocky desert inhabited by bedouins. It is punctuated by
several wadis and rises to a plateau (3,000 ft) in the Rutba region near
the border with Jordan.

Climate

Except for spring and autumn, in particular the months of April and
November, the weather is very hot and dry. In the south, however, it is
hot and wet, especially in summertime. Temperature differences
between night and day can be extreme.

In Baghdad, temperatures average about 105°F/40°C in the summer
and about 40°F/5°C in winter. From December to February, there is
frequent rain. Even snow is possible. In July and August, highs of 120°F
are common, though the low humidity makes the heat almost bearable.
In such times, Iraqis who don't have air-conditioning sleep on the

rooftops; many houses have underground living quarters, too.

In Mosul, it is also extremely hot in the summer. Winter is colder, but shorter, and frosts are frequent. On the other hand, the months of March and April, and October and November, are so pleasant that Mosul is known as the "City of Two Springs."

In the north, the mountains of Kurdistan, with elevations of over 10,000 feet (3,700 m), are covered with snow from December to March. At Hajj Omran, near the Iranian border, there is even a ski resort. In this region, temperatures remain pleasant all summer at mid-altitude.

Population

Eighty-five percent of Iraq's 23 million people are Arabs, according to a recent census. Roughly 3.4 million people belong to minorities whose cultural identity usually stems directly from their religious beliefs. The majority of even these minorities think of themselves as Arabs, including most of Iraq's 800,000 Christians, who live in Baghdad and the foothills of Kurdistan.

Kurds, the foremost ethnic minority, live mainly in the mountainous region north of the country. They number from 2 to 3 million (though unfortunately, the last official census data are from 1983). One of the most important ethnic groups in the Middle East, the Kurds are dispersed in five different countries: Iraq, Iran, Syria, Armenia, and Turkey, where the majority live. Their total population is thought to be about 25 million, which is more than Iraq's entire population (and more than the population of Armenia and Syria combined). Descendants of the Medes or Scythians, Aryan peoples who arrived in what is now Iranian Kurdistan in the first millennium BCE, the Kurds participated in the destruction of Nineveh by Nebuchadnezzar in 612 BCE, then migrated to central Anatolia (Turkey). The Kurds are mostly Sunni Muslims, like most Arabs.

The Kurdish language is related to Farsi, the language spoken in Iran; both, unlike Arabic, are Indo-European languages. Yet Kurdish is written in the Arabic alphabet, as are Farsi and Urdu (one of the principal languages of Pakistan and India).

The Kurds of Iraq have enjoyed a certain degree of autonomy on paper since the law that formed the Kurdish Autonomous Region took effect in 1974 in the governorates of Erbil, Sulaimaniya, and Dohuk, where they form the majority (see Chapter 19). Yet the reality on the ground is that the conflict between Baghdad and the Kurds has never ended; they have suffered severe repression. They remained, throughout the rule of Saddam Hussein, probably the most actively resistant of Iraq's minorities.

More mysterious is the origin of Iraq's 200,000 Yezidis, who live in the Sinjar Mountains southwest of Mosul and in Kurdistan and claim a similar Aryan inheritance to the Kurds (see Chapter 19). And then there are the 20,000 Sabeans, also called Mandeans, whose ancestors were perhaps members of an ancient Mesopotamian sect, persecuted in Palestine before the rise of Christianity (see Chapter 5). Many Sabeans are goldsmiths in Baghdad; others live in the Basra region in the South.

The Turkomans (or Turkmen), a Central Asian people, arrived in Iraq well before the Ottoman Turks. They are such an important minority in the Mosul region and Kirkuk (thought to be about 100,000 strong) that the Turkish government has considered these cities to be rightfully theirs ever since the end of World War I and the dismantling of the Ottoman Empire. (Try telling that to a Kurd, though.)

Other minorities are represented by less than a thousand people. There is a tight-knit Armenian community of a few hundred souls, the descendants of refugees from the 1915 genocide, and even fewer Mazdeans (Zoroastrians) and members of the Baha'i faith. As for the Jews, whose community was once the largest in the Middle East, they number very few today.

The southern swamp region is inhabited by the "People of the Marshes," whose ancient way of life has all but disappeared due to the draining of the swamps (see Chapter 10).

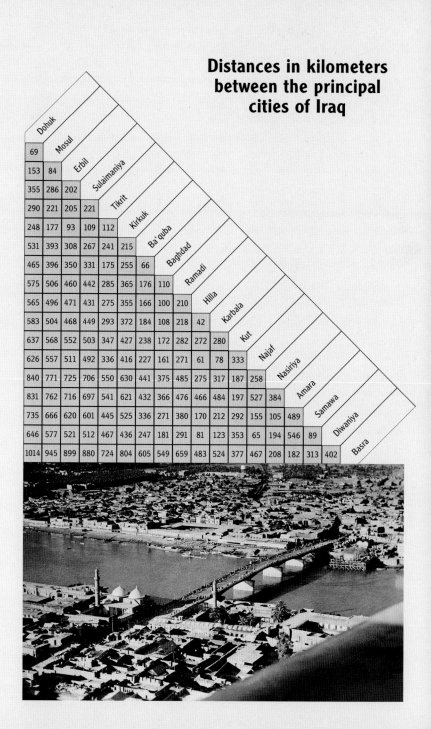

Distances in kilometers between the principal cities of Iraq

	Dohuk	Mosul	Erbil	Sulaimaniya	Tikrit	Kirkuk	Ba'quba	Baghdad	Ramadi	Hilla	Karbala	Kut	Najaf	Nasiriya	Amara	Samawa	Diwaniya
Mosul	69																
Erbil	153	84															
Sulaimaniya	355	286	202														
Tikrit	290	221	205	221													
Kirkuk	248	177	93	109	112												
Ba'quba	531	393	308	267	241	215											
Baghdad	465	396	350	331	175	255	66										
Ramadi	575	506	460	442	285	365	176	110									
Hilla	565	496	471	431	275	355	166	100	210								
Karbala	583	504	468	449	293	372	184	108	218	42							
Kut	637	568	552	503	347	427	238	172	282	272	280						
Najaf	626	557	511	492	336	416	227	161	271	61	78	333					
Nasiriya	840	771	725	706	550	630	441	375	485	275	317	187	258				
Amara	831	762	716	697	541	621	432	366	476	466	484	197	527	384			
Samawa	735	666	620	601	445	525	336	271	380	170	212	292	155	105	489		
Diwaniya	646	577	521	512	467	436	247	181	291	81	123	353	65	194	546	89	
Basra	1014	945	899	880	724	804	605	549	659	483	524	377	467	208	182	313	402

Languages

Arabic is the official language, but other languages are recognized, such as Kurdish, Turkmen (closely related to Turkish), and Syriac, or Aramaic (the language spoken by Christ).

English is the most commonly spoken foreign language, though since the Ba'ath Party's takeover in 1968, French has been taught in public schools.

Religions

Over 90 percent of Iraqis are Muslims, divided into two major groups: Sunni and Shi'a, the largest of which is Shi'a.

The Sunni (from the Arabic word for tradition, *sunna*) recognize the legitimacy of the caliphate; in other words an orderly succession of religious leaders determined by consensus.

The Shi'a Muslims (*shi'a*, from the word for "partisan") hold to the belief that the line of succession must be traced from the Prophet's family. They do not recognize the caliphs of the Umayyad and Abbasid dynasties. After the death of Mohammad's son-in-law Ali, religious authority was transmitted through imams (people whose knowledge of the Qur'an and whose behavior are judged to be exemplary). The Shi'a faith has divided into three groups, each recognizing the legitimacy of a different number of imams. The predominant group, who live in Iran and Iraq, recognizes the first twelve imams. The last Imam, who disappeared in Samara, is supposed to return at the end of time. The Septimites, or Ismailis, recognize only seven imams. Agha Khan is their leader. The Zaydites recognize only five imams. Back in 713, they refused to follow Imam Mohammed al-Bakr at the death of Imam Ayn, preferring instead his brother, Zayd (whence their name). They are more numerous in Yemen than in Iraq.

Roughly five percent of Iraqis are Christians. Many sects are represented, including Greek Orthodox or Melchites (Christians, generally from Syria and Egypt, who remained faithful to Byzantium at the Council of Chalcedonia in 451), Greek Catholic, Armenian, Protestant, as well as Chaldean, Nestorian, and Jacobite sects. The vast majority of Iraqi Christians (80 percent) are Nestorian or Chaldean.

The Nestorian Church gives precedence to Christ's human, rather than his divine, nature. Its name comes from the sect's founder, Nestorius, who was condemned by the Council of Ephesus in 413. The Nestorians' influence spread all the way to China, where they played an important role at the court of the Mongols, during their invasion of Persia and Iraq. Indeed, the Mongols almost converted to Christianity, but the Pope refused, horrified at the power the Nestorian heresy could thus have acquired. The Mongol chiefs finally opted for Buddhism or Islam, according to the peoples they ruled over. The Nestorians finally lost their influence, and were decimated by Tamerlane, the Muslim. They took refuge in Kurdistan.

The Chaldean sect has its origin in a schism with the Nestorians that occurred in 1552, led by John Sulaka. It recognizes the authority of the Pope, but retains its own rites, involving an altar facing East, and an altar called the *bema*, which symbolizes the place where Jesus prayed. Its headquarters is in Baghdad, where it is represented by the Patriarch of Babylon.

The Yezidis, who claim direct descent from Adam, are difficult to place in any category. Their religion contains elements of Christianity, Islam, and Judaism.

Finally, two extremely ancient religious minorities are active in Iraq: the Sabeans or Mandeans (followers of St. John the Baptist, who baptized Jesus), and the Mazdeans or Zoroastrians, who follow the teachings of Zarathustra.

— TWO —

Thousands of Years of History

Dust thou art, and unto dust shalt thou return.
—*Genesis 3:19*

For peoples of the Book—Christians, Jews, and Muslims—Mesopotamia (in Greek, "land between the rivers"), is part of the Holy Land, and the biblical Eden was situated in southern Iraq, between the Tigris and the Euphrates Rivers. In ancient times, the two rivers flowed into the Persian Gulf separately, about 12 miles (19 km) apart. Now they join together in the much-disputed Shatt al-Arab, which makes part of the Iran–Iraq border. Just north of their confluence, near Kurna, grows a sacred, ancient tree called "Adam and Eve's Tree." Here is the place where God told Adam and Eve, "In sorrow shalt thou eat of it all the days of thy life" (Genesis 3:17).

Indeed, the story of the human presence in Mesopotamia is long and at least as full of sorrow as triumph. The earliest traces of human presence in Mesopotamia date from the Paleolithic or Old Stone Age (25,000 to 5000 BCE). Some 6,000 years ago, before the flood, the al-Obeid civilization, inventors of the first known form of writing, extended its influence from the Gulf north to the Caspian Sea (present-day northern Iran). From that point on, many of humanity's most precious assets—ideas, arts, and technologies—began finding their way from Mesopotamia to Europe and to the rest of the world. Our 24-hour day, our earliest writing, mathematics, and ancient stories that inspired parts of the Old Testament are but a few examples.

Many great civilizations have prospered and ultimately turned to dust in Mesopotamia, under the onslaught of invading peoples. Over the centuries, the Iraqi people have been decimated by countless wars, cataclysms, and epidemics. Cities and monuments have been destroyed, restored, destroyed again, rebuilt again...and again. New cities were built to house the capitals of kings, caliphs, imams, or presidents. The history of Iraq's leaders is a bloody one, replete with plots and assassinations, often within royal families. The United States may be a relatively recent enemy for Iraq, but invasions are nothing new: the first war with the US (January 16–March 3, 1991) began on the same day as the pillage of Baghdad by the Mongols 733 years earlier.

As the rumble of yet another war clears in Iraq, it is fitting, perhaps, to reflect on all the earlier civilizations who invaded or settled, who ruled, and who finally fell from power in this ancient land. Later chapters will travel across the country, noting ruins and relics and places and features of geography that played a part in this history. But first, this chapter will serve as a truncated history—a summary of nearly 7,000 years of civilization.

Sumer: 4500 BCE–2340 BCE

This illustrious civilization began with the conquest of southern Mesopotamia, the Shinar Plain, by a people whose origins are steeped in myth. According to some accounts, they were Aryans from India who came to Mesopotamia by boat, with their culture already fully developed. A Babylonian legend portrays them as half-man, half-fish; fierce invaders under the orders of a certain Oannis, who some have linked to the prophet Jonas. (Or Youness, whose tomb is located in the hills above Mosul.)

Part of a Sumerian harp discovered in Ur

The Sumerian civilization was at its apogee for more than a millennium, between 3500–2350 BCE. During this period, Mesopotamia underwent enormous changes. Land was put to use through an intricate system of irrigation canals and with agricultural knowledge that produced an improved, iron plow. Architecture and building techniques were so advanced that the Sumerian people enjoyed a network of roughly a dozen city-states (Eridu, Ur, Uruk, Lagash, Larsa, and others), whose ruling dynasties competed for economic, political, and cultural primacy. Sumerian scholars invented cuneiform writing and mathematics, and were the first to codify square and cubic roots. It is not surprising that Sumerian goods and knowledge spread throughout the Middle East and beyond. Even in their present condition, the ruins of these great cities are ample proof of the influence and domination exercised by the world's first empire. And there is just as ample evidence of the subtlety and depth of its culture in the artistic treasures found in the royal tombs at Ur, or the epic poem of Gilgamesh (see Chapter 12), two of the most treasured legacies of Sumer.

Akkad & the Rebirth of Sumer: 2340 BCE–about 2000 BCE

The Sumerians eventually fell under the repeated onslaughts of the Akkadians, a nomadic people of Semitic origin, whom Arabs believe to be their ancestors. Sargon I, their powerful monarch, transformed Mesopotamia into a unified, centralized state, and founded a dynasty in the process—the first of the region's many. Under Sargon's rule, the demographic center of gravity shifted eastward, from the Euphrates to the Tigris—much as it remains in modern Iraq. Sargon's successors built an empire that stretched from the Taurus Mountains of Anatolia in the north and the Mediterranean to the west, to the Zagros Mountains of Persia in the east.

Around 2100 BCE, the Sumerians, led by Ur-Nammu, succeeded in wresting the independence of several city-states, notably Ur, from Akkadian rulers, who decided to maintain friendly relations with Sumer. Ur-Nammu went on to found the Third Dynasty of Ur, and proclaimed himself King of Sumer and Akkad.

The Elamites: circa 2000 BCE

This ancient people arrived in the region around the same time as the Sumerians, but occupied present-day Khuzistan, in southern Iran. For centuries they had coveted the riches of Sumer, then of Akkad. In 2003 BCE, they overthrew the already weakened Third Dynasty of Ur. This date signals the end of Sumerian cultural dominance, if not its influence.

During this period, the Amorites, a Semitic people who had infiltrated the region from the northwest, gained control of Babylon under the leadership of Sumuabom.

The Babylonians: 1760–1595 BCE

The Amorite kings succeeded in unifying all the city-states of Mesopotamia under their authority. Babylon became an important city, and the Elamites were ousted from the region. Under the rule of Hammurabi (1792–1750 BCE) and his successors, the capital became the economic and religious center of an empire that would have an influence just as tremendous as its Sumerian predecessors (without whose crucial contributions, it might be added, their success would have been impossible). He made Marduk, pictured as a horned dragon, the divinity of the Babylonian Empire, and left behind a highly elaborate code of laws. The Hammurabi Code covered all levels of human interaction: commercial, civil, and criminal, and became the basis of modern law.

In spite of the Babylonians' strengths, the region was the theater of constant wars, sparked by the ups and downs of competing dynasties, and pressures from peoples from all over the Middle East. All were covetous of Mesopotamia's riches and fertile soil. Indeed, Hammurabi had to deal with numerous threats. In 1761 BCE, the statue of Marduk was stolen during a raid by a band of Hittites, a Semitic people from Anatolia. The Kassites, a people from the Zagros Mountains of Persia, brought it back, and ended up governing Babylon for more than five centuries.

The Kassites worshipped Marduk, the divinity that inspired the Enuma Elish, one of the most important extant literary works of the period. This creation epic, in which Marduk triumphs over the forces of chaos, is said to have inspired the authors of the Old Testament.

Marduk fell again into enemy hands when the Elamites took over again in 1157 BCE, ending the Kassites' long reign. Nineteen miles (30 km) outside Baghdad, in Aqarquf, the ruins of the ziggurat, or Mountain of God, a series of edifices of three to seven levels of increasing size, leading to a temple at the summit, built in 1500 BCE, are the only visible remains of the Kassites' architectural achievements (see Chapter 6).

The Assyrians: circa 1830 BCE, then 827–612 BCE

For 3,000 years, northern Iraq had been occupied by the Assyrians, a Semitic people who had successively absorbed Sumerian and Akkadian influences. Not powerful enough to remain independent, they had been overrun by Hittites, Sumerians, Akkadians, and Babylonians. But, by joining the invaders' armies and participating in their campaigns, the Assyrians became confident enough to rid themselves of the colonizers, finally attacking and destroying Babylon. By the eighth century BCE, the Assyrians were masters of a vast territory, stretching all the way to Phoenicia on the Mediterranean coast (present-day Lebanon).

Two hundred years later, Babylon recovered some of its former strength. With the help of the Medes, an Aryan people from Persia, they avenged the destruction of their city by taking and destroying Nineveh, capital of Assyria, in 612 BCE.

The Neo-Babylonian Empire: 792–595 BCE

After his success as commander-in-chief of the Babylonian troops in the war against the Assyrians, Nabuchadnezzar II (605–562 BCE), son of Nabopolassar, was able to create a new empire that restored the glory of ancient Babylon. Science and literature flourished in an age preoccupied with the stars: astrology was invented, and, more generally, all the

Ziggurat of Aqarquf

divinatory arts. Neo-Babylonian scholars, the first astronomers, also postulated the existence of planets. Mathematicians invented algebra and theorems that were later attributed to Euclid and Pythagoras. From the Neo-Babylonians, we get our division of the day into 24 hours, of an hour into 60 minutes, and of a sphere into 360 degrees.

Nabuchadnezzar II destroyed Jerusalem in 586 BCE, and deported the Jews to Babylon, where they wrote the Hebrew Bible, drawing heavily on Mesopotamian narratives.

The Medes didn't abide for long by their accord with the Babylonians. After Nabuchadnezzar II's death, Cyrus Achemenides, King of the Persians and the Medes, took Babylon, without bloodshed for once, in 539 BCE, thanks to betrayals from within the Babylonian camp.

Babylonian lion fresco, the National Museum

The Mede and Persian Occupation: 539–330 BCE

Initially, the Babylonians were treated with understanding. The Jews, who had facilitated the Persians' entry into the city, were rewarded with their freedom. Although many returned to Palestine, many also remained in Mesopotamia.

In 521 BCE, after the death of King Darius I, his son Xerxes (486–565 BCE) succeeded to the throne. The Babylonians attempted to regain their independence, but an insurrection was brutally crushed. The Persians had Marduk's statue melted down, and Xerxes imposed Zoroastrianism as the official religion. Mesopotamia became more and more the victim of abusive taxation, and slid into poverty. The irrigation canals that had been the pride of their builders millennia ago were in such disrepair that Alexander the Great and his army were received as liberators.

The Macedonian Era: 331–129 BCE

In 331 BCE, Alexander the Great inflicted a crushing defeat on Darius III at Gaugameles, in the Erbil plain. His entrance into Babylon was triumphant, as was his project to make the city the capital of his Eastern Empire. He offered a sacrifice to Marduk, and had all the temples and sanctuaries destroyed by the Persians rebuilt. Fourteen thousand Macedonians and an equal number of Babylonian women were married in what is still probably the largest mass wedding the world has ever known. By this grandiose gesture, Alexander intended to spread the message of *oikumene* (whence comes our word "ecumenical," which means "all-inclusive"), or the union of Mediterranean and Middle Eastern peoples. Alexander went on to conquer new lands to the east: from Susa along the coast of southern Persia, to the Indus valley in what is now Pakistan. He died of a fever nine years later, back in Babylon.

After a period of uncertainty, the warlord Seleucos brought the region under control. He took the title of Nicator (the Victorious) and founded the Seleucid dynasty (312–249 BCE). In 307 BCE, he built his capital, Seleucia, on the Tigris, south of present-day Baghdad.

Under Seleucid rule, Mesopotamia flourished again. As for the Greeks, they derived enormous benefit from contact with

Mesopotamia, and appropriated the discoveries of conquered peoples as their own, making a great leap forward in the process. Needless to say, the borrowing of Babylonian culture by the Greeks brought many Babylonian ideas and inventions to Rome, and eventually to all of Europe.

The Parthian Kingdom: 129 BCE–234 CE

Taking advantage of the decline of the Seleucids, the Parthians, from northern Persia (present-day Khorassan), progressively invaded Mesopotamia, and founded the city of Ctesiphon, facing Seleucia on the opposite side of the Tigris. The Macedonians, defeated in 129 BCE, left the region, with no hope of returning. In northern Iraq, the city of Hatra declared its independence. The Parthians decided to leave in place the Arab emirs who had made Hatra their capital, on the condition that they defend the western border against what were now Roman aggressors.

Indeed, from their Syrian outposts, the Romans dreamed of restoring Alexander's Eastern Empire. They attacked Ctesiphon several times, but Parthian cavalry out-maneuvered the Roman troops commanded by General Crassus. The Roman emperor, Trajan, succeeded in taking the city, but not in keeping it. Emperor Caracalla attempted diplomacy by asking for the hand of the daughter of Artaban IV (216–224 CE), but he was rebuffed. Humiliated, Caracalla had all the royal tombs at Erbil desecrated and the remains of kings and queens scattered about. As for Artaban, he was killed in battle in 224 CE by a Persian prince, Ardachir, who went on to found his own dynasty.

The Sassanid Dynasty: 224–636 CE

After taking over Ctesiphon, Ardachir had Seleucia rebuilt and rebaptized it with his own name. He also had another city, which he called Behirsir, built next to it. His son and successor Shapur I (241–272 CE) regained control of Hatra, which had been too independent for his taste, and had it burned to the ground. Shapur I imposed Mazdeism as the official religion.

In 363, his great-grandson Shapur II (310–379) crushed the Romans, who had attacked Ctesiphon. The Emperor Julian, critically wounded, died during the retreat, somewhere near Samara.

Under Chosroes I (531–579), the Sassanids occupied Yemen, and ravaged Palestine and Syria. Chosroes II (590–628) captured Jerusalem in 614, and also took Christ's cross. He had a huge palace built at Ctesiphon, whose famous arch, one hundred feet high, is still standing.

But Chosroes II underestimated the importance of a new religion: Islam. When a messenger sent by the Prophet Muhammad himself summoned him to convert, the King was offended. Chosroes' response was to order the governor of Yemen to conquer Medina and capture Muhammad. Upon learning of the plan, the Prophet is said to have exclaimed: "May Allah tear his kingdom to shreds, as he did my letter!" And so it happened, in spite of Chosroes' son Kawad II, who, after inheriting the throne, reversed the order against Muhammad. It was too late: the army of Caliph Abu Bakr was at the door of his empire.

The Muslim Conquest: 638–661 CE

The Muslim army, commanded by Khalid Ibn al-Walid (to whom Mohammed had given the name Seif al-Islam, which means "sword of Islam") set up camp near Basra, on the Gulf coast, in 638. The Christian Arabs of Hira received Khalid's army with open arms, and the Muslim troops flew on to a string of victories.

In 637, the Arab warlord Saad al-Waqqas defeated the Persians at al-Qadisiyya, some 20 miles from Hira, in spite of being outnumbered by his adversaries, who used elephants in battle. He went on to take Ctesiphon, ending the first occupation of Mesopotamia by the Persians.

The theological disputes and internecine strife that followed Muhammad's death did not leave Iraq untouched. The election of Ali, the Prophet's son-in-law, to the position of fourth Caliph was contested by Muawiya, governor of Syria, who accused Ali of having ordered the murder of Caliph

Saad Ibn Abi al-Waqqas

Othman, his relative. The two clans faced off in 657 at Sirffin, west of Raqqa, in Syria. Neither side was able to take the advantage, so Muawiya had his soldiers spike the tips of their lances with pages of the Qur'an, and the fighting stopped. Ali accepted that the feud be taken under arbitration and, awaiting the verdict of the judges, retreated to Kufa, a city built on the Euphrates, in southern Iraq, at the edge of the desert. But a group of his partisans, who wanted to continue fighting, revolted against their chief, branding him a traitor; in 661, Ali was assassinated at Kufa by a Kharijite (secessionist) armed with a poisoned sword. His son, Hassan, succeeded him, but not for long: Muawiya, who had had himself proclaimed Commander of the Believers at Damascus, convinced him to abdicate.

Ali's partisans refused to recognize Muawiya as Caliph, and went to Medina to ask Hussein, the murdered Caliph's second son, to take up the challenge.

Upon the death of Muawiya in the spring of 680, his son Yazid succeeded him. Hussein chose this moment to act, and set out for Kufa where reinforcements were supposed to be waiting. Instead, he was ambushed and murdered, near Karbala. Subsequently, Iraq again came under Syrian domination.

The Umayyad Dynasty: 680–750 CE

The Syrian Umayyads never succeeded in winning over the Iraqi people, for they ruled in a tyrannical and chaotic manner, and repressed countless revolts in blood. Yussuf al-Hajjaj, appointed governor of the region in 694, reinforced Syrian authority using all available means, including purging the Qur'an of any sura, or verse, that could be taken as a call to overthrow the Umayyad conquerors. In 702, he built the new city of Wasit (east of Kufa, near the Tigris) to administer Iraq more closely. After his death in 714, al-Hajjaj's tomb was left unmarked to avoid its being desecrated by his many enemies.

Hatred of the Umayyads brought the Iraqi people together. Abu al-Abbas al-Saffah, a descendant of Abbas, Muhammad's uncle, was able to take advantage of the situation.

The Abbasid Dynasty: 750–1258

At Khorassan, Abu al-Abbas took the head of an army rebelling against the Syrians. The insurgents, galvanized by a brilliant Muslim propagandist, Abu Muslim ("Father of Islam"), crushed the Umayyad troops and marched on Kufa. He sent the following message to the inhabitants of the city: "The time of Allah has come! Prepare yourselves, for I am the one who sheds blood!" The city was taken without difficulty in September 749. Abu al-Abbas established his headquarters at al-Anbar, on the banks of the Euphrates, as much for the climate as for strategic reasons.

Having proclaimed himself Caliph, Abu al-Abbas had all the members of the opposing dynasty murdered, which earned him the nickname "Bloodthirsty." The only one to escape was Prince Abdurahman Ibn Muawiya. He managed to get all the way across North Africa to Spain, where the Umayyads, who were a powerful force there, elected him Emir of Cordoba in 756.

Upon the death of Abu al-Abbas in 750, Abu Muslim forced his brother to take the head of the Caliphate, but was poorly rewarded for his zeal: Abu Jaffar, who would reign under the name al-Mansur (the Victorious) had him executed. But perhaps Abu Jaffar's most important decision was to have the new city of Baghdad built.

Al-Mehdi succeeded al-Mansur as Caliph in 775; just eleven years later, Harun al-Rashid (of Arabian Nights' fame) came to power, his mother having had her eldest son murdered. Al-Rashid appointed Yahia the Barcemide, head of a prominent Persian family that had supported his bid for the throne, as his vizier, and Yahia's son Jaffar became the new Caliph's closest friend.

But Zubayda, Harun al-Rashid's wife, hated the Barcemides, and reproached Jaffar for favoring one of the Caliph's illegitimate sons, Abdallah al-Ma'moun, over her own, al-Amin. The conflict escalated, and Zubayda maneuvered so well that the Caliph ended up executing Jaffar and sentencing his father to rot in a prison for atheists.

Aside from these royal intrigues, and in spite of interrupted relations with Umayyad Spain and a hostile dynasty in Morocco, Harun al-Rashid reestablished order in his empire, and made himself popular by crushing the Byzantines, obtaining a sizeable tribute, or tax, from the Eastern Roman Empire.

When Harun al-Rashid died, his two sons went to war against each other. Al-Ma'moun, the son of a Persian slave, won out over Zubayda's son, and had him put to death in 813.

During the reigns of Harun al-Rashid (786–809) and al-Ma'moun the Great (813–833), Arab peoples in the Middle East experienced a true Golden Age. Baghdad was the center of the civilization, and the achievements of the Abbasid Muslims, both scientific and cultural, were far-reaching. The same context of prosperity and relative peace that had enabled the development of the Asian spice trade also saw the further development of science, with the invention of algebra by al-Khawarismi; of geography with the concept of a spherical earth; and of the arts, with great poets such as Abu Nawas, not to mention masters of calligraphy and illumination, musicians, and architects. Harun, a devout Muslim, made nine pilgrimages to Mecca, and was a major patron of theological research. The founders of the great schools of Islam lived in this time: Abu Hanifa, Malik Ibn Anas, Mohammad Chafei, and Ahmad Ibn Hanbal to name a few.

Although his methods were sometimes expeditious, al-Ma'moun the Great was a true intellectual. He erected a House of Wisdom with a rich library. Some of these volumes were Arabic translations of Greek, Latin, and Sanskrit works, a task that Harun al-Rashid had actively encouraged. Al-Ma'moun invited to Baghdad the learned men of the age, regardless of their religion, to enrich his people's knowledge. His support for the Mutazilites (al-Mou'tazala), who openly questioned some of the Qur'an's precepts, illustrates his open-mindedness. To stave off potential criticism from religious quarters, he won the backing of the Shi'a Muslims by proclaiming Ali (Muhammad's son-in-law, the legitimate heir to the Caliphate according to the Shi'ites) to be "the Greatest Companion after the Prophet." On his deathbed at Tus, in Persia, in 833, al-Ma'moun designated his brother, al-Mu'tassim, as his successor, and asked him to continue his work.

Al-Mu'tassim's reign (833–842) saw the increasing influence of Turkish mercenaries among the Caliph's troops. The Turks' behavior had earned the hatred of the people of Baghdad, and to escape their resentment, al-Mu'tassim eventually had a city built, Samara, which he made the new capital. But his successors would progressively succumb to the influence of the Turkish generals, even after Baghdad became the capital once again. Soon, the provincial governors were the only ones to challenge central authority, which lay in the hands of the Turks. The title Emir of Emirs was created for the most powerful among them, to fill the vacuum left by the Vizier and Caliph, whose authority was relegated to religious areas. At the death of Caliph al-Rahdi in 941, his son al-Mustaqfi (944–946) was forced to appoint a Turkish general, Kurtakin (a Daylamite, a Shi'ite tribe from the north, near the Caspian Sea) as Emir of Emirs. But the empire was quickly disintegrating into

Engraving by al-Wasiti, from the Abbasid epoch

anarchy. Ahmed Buwayhid, head of a powerful family of the region seized the opportunity. In 945, he marched on Baghdad with his brothers to reestablish order, and found a new dynasty.

The Buwayhids (945–1055)

The Buwayhid brothers obtained honorific titles and were authorized to appoint viziers. Forty days later, an argument turned bad, and Ahmed Buwayhid threw al-Mustaqfi into prison, after having his eyes gouged out. The fallen Caliph's son was placed on the throne, but the Abbasid Caliphs were now powerless.

The Buwayhids sold the empire piecemeal. Entire provinces were granted to military chieftains for services rendered. Local lords took advantage of the situation and founded ruling dynasties in Mosul, Hilla, and the lower Euphrates region. The Ayyarun, a brotherhood of bandits that thrived from the 9th to 12th centuries, became masters of Baghdad.

The Buwayhids were not able to impose their authority for long. Al-Bassassin, a former Turkish slave risen to the rank of general, had to ask the Egyptians for help in repelling the Seljuk Turk invaders. In 1046, Caliph al-Qaim (1031–1075), fearing for his life at the hands of a Fatimid caliph, an Ismailian Shi'ite, secretly established a bond with the Seljuk Turks.

The Seljuk Turks (1055–1258)

Al-Bassassin fled before the arrival of General Tughrul Beg in Baghdad in 1055. The last Buwayhid Caliph, al-Malik al-Rahim, was imprisoned. But Caliph al-Qaim quickly realized that his action had been futile. Tughrul proclaimed himself "King of al-Mashrek and al-Maghreb" (the Middle East and North Africa, respectively). Al-Qaim was forced to marry one of Tughrul's nieces, and give him the hand of one of his daughters.

Tughrul moved to Rai, in Persia, leaving a viceroy in charge of administering Iraq. At his death in 1063, his nephew Alp Arslan succeeded him, and appointed as his vizier Nizam al-Moulk, who created the Nidhamiya, one of the most prestigious schools of the age. The vizier's assassination by an Ismailian in 1092 signaled the end of the Seljuk Golden Age.

In 1118, Caliph al-Mukhtadi tried to take advantage of the chaotic situation to reassert his legitimate right to rule, but was killed by the Seljuk Sultan Massud. His son, too, was dethroned and replaced by his uncle al-Muqtafi (1136–1169). The new Caliph succeeded in liberating Hilla, Wasit, and Basra. But it took until 1186 for the Abbasids, under the leadership of al-Nasr (1180–1225) to finally rid themselves of the Seljuk Turks, whose empire was in any case disintegrating rapidly, after a long period of decline partly due to the Crusades.

His successor, al-Mustansir, created the Mustansiriya, a school that still stands (despite taking a hit in the recent war) on the banks of the Tigris in Baghdad. This Caliph was indeed better suited for architecture than for politics, and underestimated the threat posed by the Tartars, who had begun incursions in Khuzistan in 1237. His son, al-Mu'tassim (1242–1258), an incompetent ruler, stood by as the Mongols entered Baghdad, for he had not taken adequate measures for the defense of the city. He was to be the last of the Abbasid Caliphs.

The Ilkhanids (1258–1334)

By the time Genghis Khan died in 1227, the Mongols found themselves masters of almost all of Asia, and had substantial forces already massed in northern Persia. The empire had been divided among three of his sons and Tului, his grandson, with the goal of conquering new territory. In 1251, one of Tului's sons, Mongke, became Khan, and ordered his brothers, Kublai and Hulagu, to conquer new territory. While Kublai was ruling in China, Hulagu ravaged Persia, and penetrated into Iraq in 1258. He was encouraged to do so by Caliph al-Mu'tassim's vizier, Ibn al-Alkami, a Shi'ite: he thought the Mongols would place a descendant of Ali on the throne.

Baghdad resisted for a month. Al-Mu'tassim was strangled and his family eliminated. The city was given over to pillage and fire, but somehow, in spite of the estimated 800,000 dead, escaped total destruction. The great mosque and Imam Mussa al-Khadim's sanctuary were destroyed, and the books in the House of Wisdom were thrown into the Tigris. A shaykh recounted later how the water was black with ink and ashes, and it is said that the pile of burned manuscripts was so high in the river that the Mongol cavalry was able to ride across the river as over a bridge. Only the Nestorian Christians escaped the slaughter, for Hulagu's mother was a Nestorian, as were his counselors and his favorite wife.

The Mongol invasion was a great tragedy for the Arabs. Entire regions turned to dust, when the irrigation system in place since Sumerian times, millennia earlier, was destroyed. Before leaving Baghdad for other conquests, Hulagu named a governor, and appointed al-Alkami as vizier. The Mongol administrator had mosques rebuilt, and reestablished order and economic activity.

At Hulagu's death in 1265, his son, Aba Qakhan, a Buddhist, vowed to consolidate his father's work. Contacts were made with the Crusaders in view of mounting a campaign against Egypt, but the project never materialized, doubtless due to the Pope's mistrust of the Nestorians and fear of their eventual influence.

Takudar Khan ascended the throne in 1282. He converted to Islam, restored the Shaykh Ma'ruf Mosque in Baghdad, and returned religious treasures that had been taken from the Muslims. In 1295, after a period of political turmoil, Sultan Ghazan, a Muslim, had a new system of irrigation canals built, contributing to the prosperity of the region between the Euphrates and Karbala. After his death in 1304, the Ilkhanid dynasty entered its decline. Iraq fell to the hands of rebel factions. One of them, led by General Hassan Burzug al-Jalairi, prevailed.

The Jalairid Dynasty: 1334–1410

Hassan Burzug continued to consider the Mongols to be the legitimate sovereigns of the country. When he died in 1356, his son Awais managed to conquer Azerbaijan, a region northwest of Iran. In his absence, the acting Caliph, a captain named Marjan, attempted to take power. Upon Awais' return, the traitor was arrested, and curiously, pardoned. He built the mosque and caravanserai that bear his name in Baghdad.

From 1374 on, Iraq was attacked by the Turkomans. First, by a tribe based in the region of Lake Van, just north of Iraq in Anatolia, known for the black sheep on their flag and on the burial stones of their chiefs. The province of Mosul was taken by Qaraquryenli.

Tamerlane, a Turkoman prince from Samarkand, attacked Baghdad for the first time twenty years later, without causing too much damage. Hassan, the Sultan, had preferred to flee. Tamerlane went on to seize and destroy Tikrit and Mosul, cities that had dared to put up a resistance, then headed toward Anatolia. But, upon learning that Hassan had returned to Baghdad, he turned around, and this time, in 1401, destroyed the city. His soldiers, each of whom was to cut two heads, brought back 90,000 altogether, and arranged them in 120 pyramids.

Tamerlane died in 1405, after having decided to rebuild Baghdad. Hassan attempted in vain to recover his lost empire. He took Tabriz in Azerbaijan, but was himself made prisoner and executed.

The Black Sheep Dynasty (Qara-Koyunlu): 1410–1467

In 1411, Shah Mohammad, chief of the arrestingly-named Black Sheep tribe, had just ascended the throne of Baghdad when his brother, Isfahan, had him murdered and usurped the throne. Some years later, his son, Jihan (1439–1467) replaced him. In 1466, he launched a campaign against Hassan Beg Tawil, chief of the White Sheep, his ancestral enemies, based in Diyarbakir (in Anatolia). The operation failed miserably, and Jihan Shah died in the fighting. One of his sons, who had become chief, committed suicide upon realizing he could not win the war. Thus ended the short-lived reign of the Turkoman Black Sheep in Iraq.

The White Sheep Dynasty (Aq-Koyunlu): 1467–1509

Hassan Beg Tawil chose Tabriz, in Persia, as his capital. At his death, his sons became locked in a struggle for succession; in 1499, Murad Beg prevailed. He, however, lost Azerbaijan in 1503 after being defeated by Shah Ismail, a Safavid, and took refuge in Baghdad. He died in 1509, and his dynasty with him. The Pope was not happy, since he was counting on the White Sheep to contain the Ottomans, who were becoming an ever more threatening presence.

Today, the Turkomans living in Iraq in the region around Kirkuk and Tell Afar are for the most part descendants of the Black Sheep and White Sheep tribes.

The Safavid Dynasty: 1509–1534

The Safavids' origin is uncertain. Said to be of Turkoman or Kurdish affiliation, they claim as their ancestor Safi al-Din (died 1334), a Sufi shaykh from Azerbaijan, whose religious order had evolved from Sunni to an ascetic form of Shi'a Islam. The word "Sufi" comes from the Arabic for wool, which was their preferred garb. Sufis believe in gaining an experiential knowledge of God, based on the teachings of Muhammad. Their dogma is transmitted from shaykh to shaykh within each Sufi brotherhood. The head of the Safavids affirmed the divine nature of Safi al-Din, and claimed that he was the earthly representative of the Twelfth Imam, who had mysteriously disappeared at Samara.

Shah Ismail took Baghdad without bloodshed in 1508, but his fanatical troops massacred the Sunni Muslims, and destroyed the tombs of Abu Hanifa and Abdelkader al-Guilani (see Chapter 4). Shi'a was declared the official form of Islam. The Shah appointed a viceroy and returned to Persia after accomplishing a pilgrimage to Karbala and Najaf, the two most holy cities for Shi'ites, where the sons of Ali, Hassan and Hussein, had died.

The Safavid reign in Iraq was a short one. Upon the death of Shah Ismail in 1524, Dhul-Fiqar, the Kurdish Emir of Luristan, (mountainous region north of Khuzistan) seized Baghdad and the other principal cities of Iraq. To protect himself against Safavid vengeance, he allied himself with the Ottoman Sultan Sulaiman the Magnificent. This did not prevent Shah Tamasib I from launching a punitive expedition against Baghdad in 1530 and executing the rebel emir.

The Ottoman Empire: 1534–1915

Sulaiman the Magnificent was furious that someone had dared assassinate one of his vassal emirs. The fate of Baghdad and notably its Sunni population at the hands of the Safavids incensed him further. He prepared an expeditionary corps and made his triumphal entry into Baghdad in 1534; the Safavid viceroy had fled. For the next four hundred years—with the exception of the short time during which the Persians made a bid for power—Iraq would be an Ottoman province.

But the Turks' control did not extend beyond the big cities, and the countryside was left entirely to the great bedouin tribes.

Sulaiman the Magnificent stayed in Iraq four months, long enough to reestablish peace in the region. He went to pray over the tombs of Abu Hanifa and al-Guilani, and had their mausoleums, which had been destroyed by the Persians, rebuilt and embellished. In the years following, Ottoman governors came and went without incident, until one was assassinated in 1622. The mutineers, led by Bekr Agha, chief of police, appealed to Shah Abbas, a Safavid still on the Persian throne, but ended up concluding an agreement with Istanbul, according to which Agha was made governor of Baghdad. This infuriated Shah Abbas, who laid siege to the city. After three months, the inhabitants were reduced to cannibalism, and the Persians succeeded in gaining entry into the city with the help of the governor's son, who opened the gates. The Sunni Muslims were again massacred, and the famous tombs of Hanifa and al-Guilani desecrated once more.

Baghdad remained under Safavid control for sixteen years. According to legend, nobody dared inform the Ottoman Sultan, Murad IV, that the city had been taken over by the Persians. The news came to him through an Iraqi imam, who had obtained a post at the mosque where the Sultan went to pray. At the end of the sermon, the imam is reported to have said: "What use is it to broadcast the word of Allah and of the Prophet here? Are there still any true believers today? Where are those who take up arms in defense of the true believers? For seven years, the holy city of Baghdad has been the prey of the infamous Shi'ite. Their presence soils the glorious temples where our caliphs prayed, and no one has done anything about it. Nobody is doing anything to throw them out of the holy sanctuaries where they have desecrated our most sacred relics." Upon hearing this, the Sultan allegedly jumped on his horse, and without even returning to his palace, set up camp on the Asian side of the Bosphorus Strait, until he had assembled an army of 10,000 men to march on Baghdad.

The Ottoman army met the Safavid troops near Samara, and forced them to beat a retreat all the way to Baghdad. The city was taken on Christmas Day, after a 40-day siege. Sultan Murad IV made an impressive entry preceded by 50 Persian generals in chains. He gave orders to rebuild the destroyed sanctuaries, and left for Istanbul through the Gate of the Talisman, that he had symbolically walled so that no one after him, especially no invader, should enter Baghdad. (The Turks themselves would destroy it in 1917, during the evacuation of Iraq.)

Iraq became the "Principality of Baghdad" and the Iraqi people again saw a succession of Ottoman governors, for the most part Janissaries or Mameluks, the elite Turkish soldiers. The former were recruited by kidnapping Christian children (a decree actually forced the Christians of conquered lands to give the Ottomans one son out of five), while the latter were slaves, generally Cherkessians, Turkomans, or Mongols. These two elite corps formed a fanatically disciplined Praetorian guard.

The distance separating Baghdad and Istanbul was great enough that the Turkish pashas had free reign. Some went about bleeding the population—of its wealth, at the very least, but often literally. In 1826, Sultan Mahmud decided to eliminate the Janissaries. The Iraqi Mameluks, also a danger to the central authority, were exterminated in the courtyard of the palace in Baghdad some years later.

In 1869, the Sultan appointed Midhat Pasha to Baghdad. A man who valued good administration, Midhat renovated the legal system and security apparatus, and built schools and a hospital. He had the first printing press imported, and published Iraq's first newspaper, *al-Zawra*. Iraq was at the time administratively divided into three governorates or vilayats: Mosul, Baghdad, and Basra, which included Kuwait. After the departure of Midhat Pasha in 1872, the country fell into a state of chaos. Only in 1908, with the arrival of the "Young Turks," would hopes for autonomy be rekindled.

The revolution of the Young Turks signaled the birth of Arab nationalism in Iraq. On July 24, 1908, Ottoman officers belonging to this organization forced Sultan Abdul Hamid to agree to a constitution and a parliament. The majority faction, united under the Committee for Union and Progress (CUP), imposed a vizier of its choice, and founded a political party. In Baghdad, the CUP operated clandestinely. Ostensibly promoting democracy, the Young Turks' ideology was rather more akin to the French Jacobins in character; their real goal was the "Turkization" of minorities. Iraqi officers joined the al-Ahd Society, founded in Istanbul in 1913. One of them was Nuri Said, who would later become Prime Minister of the kingdom of Iraq, with the help of the British. Pan-Arabism was emerging, and it took hold of many anti-CUP parties.

As Iraq entered the 20th century, it was estimated to have a population of roughly 2.5 million people. Since the Mongol conquest about 650 years earlier, Iraq had lost roughly two-thirds of its population—to war, poverty, the plague, and other diseases such as cholera. Yet even in this reduced state, Iraq remained at the crossroads of world civilization, still of interest to the dying Ottoman empire, and to the British empire, too. Even before the discovery of oil.

The British Occupation and Mandate: 1914–1932

As early as 1871, a German group of experts touring the vilayat of Mosul and Baghdad had noted the abundance of petroleum deposits, describing Iraq as a veritable "lake of oil," but concluded that its extraction would not be profitable. In 1892, Lord Curzon, Viceroy of India, declared: "Baghdad, indirectly, is part of the set of ports of the Gulf. It is thus imperative for the Crown to annex the area as a zone of absolute British influence."

At this point, Great Britain had been interested in Mesopotamia for well over a century. As seems to happen with empires, the interests of a powerful company (the East India Company) had led the government to the region. The British controlled the southern route to India, which passed through the Red Sea, and the northern route through Afghanistan. But the middle road, through Baghdad, was considerably shorter.

In the 17th century, the British set up a trade outpost in Basra, and soon demanded that its agent be granted consular status. A century later, Britain was powerful enough in the region to appoint one of its protégés, Sulaiman Pasha, head of Baghdad Province. In return, the British were granted many privileges, and the "Resident" became a highly influential adviser. This setup proved to be as useful in Iraq as it was to become in India: by the early 1800s, the Resident was one of the most important men in the country. British companies, such as the

An 18th-century engraving of Baghdad

Lynch Brothers, which founded a navigation company on the Tigris in 1841, made their presence felt. The cities of Kut and Amara, supply stops for the steamers, became important cities. By late in the century, the opening of the Suez canal and the consolidation of steam navigation on the Tigris and Euphrates made the route through Iraq even more practical for the British. That, and the oil the German experts were investigating, would be hard to give up.

The Fight for Oil

Following the discovery of oil, Germany initiated its own bid for influence. Berlin appointed a consul to Baghdad in 1894, followed by another in Mosul, and Kaiser Wilhelm II started negotiating with Sultan Abdul Hamid about a Berlin–Baghdad railway with a planned spur to Basra. Germany obtained the right to conduct exploratory oil drilling on a 12-mile-wide strip of land split down the middle by the railroad.

This worried the British as much as it pleased Germany's allies, the Turks, for Basra was situated opposite the Anglo–Persian Oil Company's refinery at Abadan, downriver on the Shatt al-Arab.

Furthermore, the Germans were considering creating agricultural colonies, a project whose success would give them decisive influence in the region. But the British colonial impetus was not to be trifled with—by 1914 the government itself had a 51-percent stake in the Anglo–Persian company.

Beginning as far back as 1830, the government of British India had begun to train the Iraqi army and to carry out thorough topographical surveys. They had installed a telegraph system, and the arrival of doctors and archeologists enabled the British to make contact with all levels of Iraqi society. British spies, disguised as travellers, merchants, or archeologists, tracked German activity, catalogued the various bedouin tribes and religious communities, and established friendships with their chiefs. The data accumulated over nearly a century of reports to the Foreign Office served as the basis for a three-volume pocket guide to Iraq used by British invasion troops in 1914.

With World War I, and the declaration of hostilities against Germany and its Ottoman ally, the British quickly found invasion of Iraq to be a logical step. On November 6, 1914, an expeditionary corps debarked at the southern tip of Iraq. It quickly took Basra, Abadan (on the Persian side of the Tigris), and Nasiriya, 125 miles (201 km) inland toward Baghdad. But the push north to Baghdad was anything but easy. German secret agents had set the tribes afire. The Turks, advised by Prussian officers such as Field Marshall von der Goltz, counterattacked, surprising the British. The Anglo–Indian troops, commanded by General Townshend, had to retreat before Ctesiphon and were surrounded at Kut, 90 miles (145 km) down the Tigris. London decided to send T.E. Lawrence, who was sitting in the Cairo Intelligence Bureau, as an "archeologist," to bribe the Turks and the surrounding tribes, but these efforts were futile. On April 29, 1916, 13,000 British and Indian soldiers, 5 generals, and 476 officers surrendered at Kut after a five-month siege. General Townshend was taken prisoner, and 4,000 men died in captivity.

Two months later Sharif Hussein of Mecca called on the Arabs to revolt against the Ottomans and their German allies, putting his faith in Britain's promise of a great Arab kingdom. Humiliated by their crushing defeat, and reinvigorated by the Sharif of Mecca's support, the British sent a powerful expeditionary corps as reinforcements, under the leadership of General Stanley Maude. He swiftly navigated up the Tigris, and took Baghdad by surprise on March 11, 1917. Eight days later, he addressed a proclamation to the people—a surprising gesture on the part of an invader—in which he solemnly committed himself to the self-determination of the Iraqi people. Maude's promise would not be kept.

For although promises were being made to the Arabs—to Sharif Hussein, to Ibn Saud, to the Iraqi people—the French and the British had already concluded a secret pact of their own: the 1916 Sykes–Picot Agreement. British and French diplomats had agreed to divide up the Ottoman territories between themselves, creating respective zones of influence.

Although the vilayat of Mosul had been reserved for France in the secret plan, Maude ordered his troops to march upon the northern city anyway. Lloyd George, British Foreign Minister, asserted hypocritically that the region's oil was necessary for the Iraqi budget. In fact, he was betting on the French being amenable to negotiations, given their lesser national stake in access to oil.

On November 8, 1918, five days after the armistice with Turkey was signed, the British entered Mosul. Lloyd George began talks in London with Georges Clemenceau, the French president, debating the fate of Mosul in the context of the Sykes–Picot Agreement. By February, the French had accepted the British presence in Mosul, on condition that the French be allowed to participate in oil exploitation in the area. A year later, at the Conference of San Remo in April 1920, Great Britain easily won the power of mandate over all of Iraq.

Meanwhile, revolt was brewing in northern Mesopotamia. In May 1919, Mahmud, a Kurdish shaykh, proclaimed himself "King of Kurdistan," and took Sulaimaniya. The British bombarded his positions and used poison gas to regain control of the region. Tension escalated in all of Iraq, and the independence movement's popularity exploded. Several nationalist organizations went into hiding. Mosques and cafés became meeting places and propaganda centers. Repression of these activities was intense. Unrest rapidly spread to all levels of Iraqi society.

The Insurrection of 1920

The insurrection was triggered by the arrest of a shaykh in June 1920. The shaykh's tribe stormed the prison where their chief was being held and freed him. On July 20, the Euphrates tribes rose up and, with the revolt quickly spreading to the rest of the country, the British had to barricade themselves in Baghdad, pending the arrival of reinforcements. More than 2,000 British and Indian troops died, were injured, or disappeared. The Indian Office treated the uprising as the result of an international plot fomented by the Germans, the Kemalists (Turkish republicans), and pan-Arab groups—all manipulated by the Bolsheviks.

The Foreign Office had to act fast. Sir Percy Cox replaced Sir Arnold Wilson as high commissioner, with orders to create a viable Arab state as soon as possible. The British prepared to govern Iraq by proxy, and a temporary government was formed under the leadership of Abdel Rahman al-Guilani. Each minister was paralleled by a British counterpart, who had the real power. Jaffar al-Askari and Nuri Said, two pro-British Iraqi officers who had participated in the "Arab Revolt" led by Emir Faisal and T.E. Lawrence were recalled to Baghdad, with the former appointed head of the army and the latter, chief of police.

In March 1921, Faisal, one of Hussein's sons, was chosen as the future king of Iraq by Winston Churchill at the Conference of Cairo. Faisal had been without a throne since his expulsion from Syria by General Gouraud. The decision, supported by T.E. Lawrence and Gertrude Bell (see sidebar on next page) was kept private in order not to embarrass Faisal, who didn't want to seem to be a British puppet.

Faisal arrived in Baghdad on June 29, 1921, quasi incognito. A referendum was immediately organized, which appeared to give the new king 96 percent of the vote, and legitimized, if only in appearance, his accession to the throne. On August 23, in the courtyard of the Serai, he was crowned Faisal I, King of Iraq, by the Grace of Her Majesty, the Queen of England.

Gertrude Bell, Uncrowned Queen of Iraq

Gertrude Bell was as grand and important a figure as T.E. Lawrence ("Lawrence of Arabia"), and played a major role in the tumultuous history of the Middle East in the early 20th century. She and her destiny have, however, all but fallen into oblivion.

Her penchant for travelling in the deserts of Iraq and Arabia, where foreigners, not to mention foreign women, were rarely welcomed, had caught the eye of British intelligence before the World War I. She had even been taken prisoner for two weeks by a suspicious Arab shaykh. Back in London, her only wish was to set out again for more adventure. The outbreak of war in 1914 provided the opportunity.

British Intelligence recruited Gertrude Bell in 1915. Her unit's mission was to organize an Arab revolt against the Turks from Cairo. She frequented T.E. Lawrence, whom she had met several years before on the archeological site of Kerkemish, in Turkey, where he was overseeing the construction of the Baghdadbahn, the Berlin–Baghdad railroad.

Gertrude Bell proved her talents after her arrival in Basra in February 1916. Her perfect Arabic and her knowledge of local customs enabled her to quickly obtain support from within the Iraqi population. After the taking of Baghdad in February 1917, her influence increased. With the full backing of Winston Churchill himself, she steered Iraqi affairs from the shadows, notably countering Turkish bids for Mosul and Kirkuk. She was against an independent Kurdistan, which she believed would only fall under Turkish influence, and she worked with Lawrence to put Faisal on the throne. She also founded Iraq's first museum, true to her archeological passion.

Gertrude Bell's tomb is in Baghdad, in a small Christian cemetery. She allegedly committed suicide on July 11, 1926, disappointed at the progress of history.

The Kingdom of Iraq: 1921–1958

The crowning of Faisal I in August 1921 had, not surprisingly, provoked the anger of Iraqi nationalists. The King knew that he was not loved. In an attempt to modify his image, he appointed to the post of chamberlains two prominent Anglophobes; Faisal also supposedly secretly encouraged anti-British demonstrations.

Yet in 1922, trouble began anew. Faisal was declared ill, and Percy Cox, British High Commissioner, exerted power in his stead. Newspapers were closed down, and nationalist chiefs imprisoned or deported. Back in Sulaimaniya, the Kurdish Shaykh Mahmud took up

Faisal I

arms once again. But the British employed mercenaries, hardy Assyro-Chaldean warriors, to drive him out of the city. The Shaykh pursued his combat in the mountains until 1927, then took refuge in Persia.

Further angering the nationalists was the Anglo–Iraqi Treaty, signed on October 10, 1922. According to the terms of this treaty, Iraq could open an embassy in London, but Britain was to represent Iraq everywhere else in the world. The treaty was signed under the threat of a return to martial rule.

In 1927, an oil field of unprecedented size was discovered near Kirkuk. A year later, the Iraq Petroleum Company was constituted. France, who had created the Compagnie Francaise des Petroles, obtained 23.75 percent of future profits.

Independence on British Terms

The League of Nations admitted Iraq in October 1932. With this, the British mandate officially ceased, but not British influence. The Iraqi Army, whose officers had been trained in England or by the Ottomans, became one of the principal forces in the kingdom. In theory the army was loyal to the monarchy, and in particular to Nuri Said. Several uprisings, among the Kurds and the Assyrians (who had settled in northern Iraq, after fleeing the Mongols, who they had once helped), were swiftly crushed. But dissension eventually became evident, with the army increasingly espousing the point of view of the people.

King Faisal I died mysteriously on September 1, 1933 in a Swiss hospital. Nuri Said, with the sovereign in Switzerland, announced the news by telegram. Faisal is now interred in a Baghdad mausoleum with his family.

His popular son Ghazi took the throne under the name Ghazi I. Close to the nationalists, the young king gave the British a run for their money. Although educated in England, he nourished a deep hatred for the British, and the feeling was reciprocal. During his short reign—six years—he had to repress revolts by the Assyrians, the Kurds, and the Shi'ites. Ghazi turned to the Germans, who had a dynamic delegation in Baghdad, for help in ousting the British.

In 1936, General Bakr Sidqi, of Kurdish origin, led a coup, becoming head of the army. Jaffar al-Askari, defense minister, was assassinated,

and his brother-in-law, Nuri Said, fled to Palestine in a British plane. King Ghazi let things unfold. A temporary government was appointed, more representative than the old one. But the new regime, inspired by the Kemalists, alienated nationalists by courting the Turks and Iran, to the

Ghazi I making a radio speech from his palace calling for the "liberation" of Kuwait

detriment of Iraq's Arab neighbors. As for the Iraqi army, it was divided between a pro-Bakr faction and an Arab-nationalist faction.

On August 11, 1937, Bakr Sidqi was assassinated in Mosul. A general amnesty was declared. Rashid Ali al-Guilani, a major figure of Arab nationalism (see sidebar), now became the man to contend with.

On December 25, 1938, in a fetid atmosphere of conspiracy, the king was forced to recall Nuri Said. He dissolved the parliament, and implicated those behind Nuri's flight in a fictitious plot. On April 3, 1939, King Ghazi, whose sympathies for Germany and personal desire to absorb Kuwait into the Iraqi kingdom were well known, died in a car "accident." His son Faisal, only four at the time, ascended the throne. Although dissolved, the parliament was reconvened for the swearing-in of Emir Abdullah, one of the new king's cousins, as regent. On September 3, Great Britain declared war on Germany. Nuri Said, who had retained significant power, immediately expelled Fritz Grobba, the popular German ambassador.

Rashid Ali's Revolt

On April 1, 1941, Rashid Ali obtained the support of Hajj Amin al-Husseini, the Grand Mufti of Jerusalem, and of the colonels of the "Golden Square," a group of four powerful army officers. The four seized control of the country, and the regent Abdullah, fearing arrest, fled in the trunk of an American diplomatic vehicle, just before the Habaniyya British military base was surrounded. Parliament voted him out of power a few days later.

The German assistance the new government had hoped for never really materialized. Hitler was busy preparing the Russian campaign. Rifles and ammunition sent by the Vichy-led colonial authorities in Syria arrived too late. The British had obtained reinforcements from the Arab Legion of Glubb Pasha in Jordan, and recaptured Baghdad on May 30, 1941. The next day, the regent was back, under the hateful

Rashid Ali

eyes of the populace. Rashid Ali and the Mufti managed to escape the country, but the four colonels of the "Golden Square" were condemned to death and hanged from the gates of the Defense Ministry.

Rashid Ali's revolt nevertheless had left a profound impression on Arab nationalists. The Iraqi mutineers inspired the young Egyptian colonel Gamal Nasser, as well as other North African anti-colonialists. In 1954, Rashid Ali took refuge in Cairo, and rallied the Iraq Revolution in July 1958, making a triumphant return to Baghdad. But he had to flee once more a few months later, when General Qasim accused him of fomenting a "pro-Nasser" plot. After his death in Beirut in 1965, he was given a state funeral in Baghdad.

— THREE —

Iraq Since the Revolution of 1958

After World War II, Iraq was prey to sporadic unrest, with more or less serious incidents breaking out at regular intervals around the country. Ministers and cabinets succeeded each other without bringing any real improvement to the political climate. The accession to the throne of Faisal II on May 2, 1953 made no difference.

The Overthrow of the Monarchy

Opposition to the pro-British government of Nuri Said grew after the 1955 Baghdad Pact (an American-sponsored anti-communist alliance of a number of countries near the Soviet Union) and the tripartite British–French–Israeli invasion of Egypt in 1956. Demonstrations organized during the nationalization of the Suez Canal in 1956 grew violent, and martial law was declared in several regions, and the leaders of varied political parties were arrested.

The reign of the Hashemite family was coming to an end. On July 14, 1958, the monarchy was overthrown by army units headed by Free Officers, a fairly small group of military who had been meeting secretly. The royal family and Nuri Said were executed, and the regime's first proclamation that the army had liberated "the beloved homeland from the corrupt crew that imperialism installed" was generally met with jubilation in the streets of Baghdad and the rest of the country.

Abdel-Karim Qasim and Abdel-Salam Araf emerged as the leaders of the revolt, and Qasim became Prime Minister. The government withdrew from the Baghdad Pact and established relations with socialist countries, making clear its split from Britain and the West. But the Free Officers were not themselves of a coherent political philosophy: they wanted to overthrow the monarchy and rid the country of British influence, but once that was done, divisions within the new government grew. As in any country, these divisions might be drawn between the right (in Iraq, Arab nationalists) and the left (Iraqi nationalists and communists). Neither the Ba'athists, who were soon to emerge as a powerful group, nor the nationalists had the political clout that the Communist party (ICP) had, and so it was in that direction that Qasim began to lean, in an effort to coalesce a ruling party. By the end of the summer, a progressive program of agrarian reform was in the works, and by 1961, the Iraqi Petroleum Company (IPC) saw its royalties slashed by a big percentage.

A power struggle between Qasim and Araf grew, and what seemed most clearly to define it was a debate about whether or not to join the United Arab Republic (UAR) of Syria and Egypt. Michel Aflaq (see sidebar) came to Baghdad to push for Iraq's joining, and both the Ba'athists and the pan-Arab nationalists came together with Araf around this position. The struggle ended in the coup of February 8, 1963, in which nationalist and Ba'ath factions ousted Qasim, ironically, he had split from the communists. With the help of the United States CIA, the Ba'ath party began arresting thousands of communists and leftists; many were later tortured to death or executed. Nine months later, however, the Ba'athists were themselves forced out of power by Araf, who, along with his brother, ruled for a total of five relatively quiet years. Yet trouble was still brewing: the Kurds continued to rebel in the north, the Iraqi people were disappointed by the revolution's failure to change their lives, and the Arab world suffered the humiliating defeat in the 1967 war against Israel. Another revolution was to come.

Michel Aflaq and the Ba'athists

Michel Aflaq, the Ba'athists' ideologue, was born in 1910 in a nationalist Christian family in Damascus, Syria, which was then under Ottoman control. As a young man, he studied in Paris, where he met Salah al-Din al-Bitar. Both men became active in Arab independence movements in Paris.

Upon their return to Syria, the two assumed posts teaching at a Damascus high school, and were quickly spotted by the French authorities for their anti-colonialist activism. In 1942, they organized several demonstrations in support of Rashid Ali's revolt in Iraq, and in 1944 the two men established the Ba'ath Party, a political organization to spearhead what they thought of first and foremost as a spiritual movement, whose objectives would embrace those of the Arab world as a whole. All Arabs' lives must change, they said, to enable them to pass "from humiliation to glory, from decadence to progress." "Ba'ath" in Arabic has the double meaning of "insurrection" and "rebirth."

Michel Aflaq

The Ba'athist slogan, "One Arab nation with an eternal mission," aptly expressed the grandness of Aflaq's vision. The different Arab nations, whose frontiers were after all drawn by the colonial powers, were for the Ba'athists, simply different regions of one *umma*. Though the party's goals (unity, liberty, and socialism) were primarily secular, Islam was nevertheless the driving force behind pan-Arabism. As early as 1946, Ba'athists called for a general strike in opposition to the Anglo-American plan to install 100,000 European Jews in Palestine. "Arab governments won't save Palestine, only popular action will," said Aflaq presciently.

In February 1954, Ba'athist officers in Syria successfully carried out a coup, and two years later, al-Bitar entered the government as minister of foreign affairs. In 1958 Aflaq and al-Bitar agreed to dissolve the Syrian Ba'athist party in order to join the United Arab Republic (of Syria and Egypt, and, Aflaq soon hoped, Iraq). When relations between the two countries soured, conflict arose. Finally, a decade after rising to power, both Aflaq and al-Bitar were disowned by the new generation of Syrian Ba'athists. But the Iraqi Ba'athists, under Saddam Hussein, claimed to be faithful to the original principles of the Ba'ath Party, as it was founded by Aflaq and al-Bitar. Aflaq remained secretary general of the party until his death in 1989, when he was succeeded by Saddam Hussein.

The Revolution of July 17, 1968

Over the protests of Damascus, Ahmad Hassan al-Bakr became President of the Republic and Chief Commander of the armed forces.

At dawn on July 17, al-Bakr drove a white Mercedes toward the barracks of the Republican Guard. Behind him was a truck filled with Ba'ath Party militants including Saddam Hussein and his brother, Barzan. At the gate, an officer with Ba'athist sympathies let the convoy in. Saddam and the others immediately went into action, seizing several tanks. The assault was brief, and Araf, who was promised his life, surrendered after the first shots were fired on the Palace. Ahmad Hassan al-Bakr seized the reins of power. The Ba'athist Revolution had achieved victory, and had done so practically without a shot; for this reason it has been referred to as Iraq's "Bloodless" or "White" Revolution.

The Presidency of al-Bakr

The immediate period following the revolution was one of consolidating power for the Ba'athists. Al-Bakr was older and more experienced than any of his colleagues, so authority fell to him naturally. He had been a Free Officer, and had held military rank before the coup of 1963; he had regime-strengthening connections both within the Ba'ath party and the military.

He consolidated his power with the help of Saddam Hussein, who ably ran both the party, the state's security apparatus, and the Ba'ath militia (the National Guard). The two set about Ba'athizing the armed forces, transferring or retiring any officers whose loyalty was uncertain. By the end of the summer, the regime's first constitution was issued, declaring Islam to be the state religion; socialism its economic system; and the Revolutionary Command Council (RCC) the supreme political authority.

The early years of the regime were fraught with campaigns of terror aimed at consolidating power and making clear the regime's steady opposition to Britain (first and foremost), the United States, and its Middle East allies Israel and Iran. Not surprisingly, it sought to ally itself with the Soviet Union and other socialist countries. And it must be said that the show trials and the terror campaigns that took place were part, not the whole, of the regime's program. It prided itself on being a "progressive" regime, with the nationalization of the country's oil fields a top priority, and a relatively early success. For the first time, Iraq controlled the entirety of its own oil resources, and at last had the means to begin to modernize. Agrarian reform continued with considerable success, and the Ba'ath party seemed eager to address many of the social concerns that had once been the province of the communists: better education and health care, a more just allocation of resources, and so forth.

Another early success story was the regime's series of negotiations with the Kurds, led by Mustafa Barzani, which concluded in a 1970 manifesto recognizing the Kurdish nationality and language and establishing an autonomous region in northern Iraq (see Chapter 19).

Yet all was not what the Ba'athists seemed to make it. At the same time the regime pursued social policies formerly linked to the communists, thousands of individual communists were arrested and tortured to death. A great divide existed between the government's socialist aspirations and pursuit of foreign allies such as the USSR and its relations with Iraqi communists and other dissidents.

The early 1970s, with its boom in oil prices following the 1973 Arab–Israeli war, brought sudden enormous wealth to Iraq, and the regime was able to initiate major development projects and reforms in all areas. Yet trouble still brewed: in the Kurdish north, with Iran (despite the Algiers Accord of 1975), and in its domestic politics.

Saddam Hussein in Charge

On July 16, 1979, in ill-health, President al-Bakr announced his resignation and officially bestowed supreme executive authority upon Saddam Hussein, whose qualities of "courage and integrity" he extolled. Saddam Hussein, who had been his partner from the start, was the obvious choice. His tenure in the number two position had prepared him for government. But this prospect was not to everyone's liking.

With Saddam Hussein's arrival at the summit of power, Iraq entered a new era, characterized by accelerated development in all areas of Iraqi society. This development would soon be all but halted

Saddam Hussein's Rise to Power

Saddam Hussein's official biography reads like a cross between the Horatio Alger story favored by many American politicians (the humble roots, the bootstraps) and an adventure story full of clandestinity, violence, and betrayal.

He was born fatherless to a family of poor peasants on April 28, 1937 at al-Owja, a village near Tikrit in northern Iraq. His family tree traces his genealogy back to the Imam Ibn Abi Taleb, son-in-law of Mohammed and the fourth Caliph of Islam. When he was very young, his mother remarried (her dead husband's brother, according to custom) and the family moved to al-Showesh, a miserable village far from Tikrit. Saddam Hussein would doubtless have led a peasant's existence, like his parents, if his young cousin, Adnan Kayralla (the future defense minister) hadn't encouraged him to go to school. After trying in vain to convince his parents to let him enroll, at age eight, Saddam ran away from home, with a gun stuffed into his coat. A relative, worried for the boy's safety in a dangerous country, had loaned him the weapon.

In Tikrit, his maternal uncle, Kayralla Tolfah, took him under his wing. Tolfah, who had studied to become a teacher, had later joined the army, and as an officer, had participated in the 1941 anti-British coup led by Rashid Ali. Arrested and banned from the army, he had been sentenced to five years in prison. He became Saddam's guardian, seeing to his education, both in school and in the politics of nationalism.

After obtaining his secondary diploma at the al-Kharkh School in Baghdad, Saddam was aroused to militancy during the great anti-colonialist and anti-monarchist demonstrations. In 1956, after the Franco–British assault on Suez, Saddam joined the Ba'ath Party.

After the overthrow of the monarchy, Saddam Hussein, who was suspected of having assassinated a partisan of Qasim in Tikrit, was imprisoned for six months, then acquitted. He became popular in the party, and upon his return to Baghdad, Party leaders selected him to participate in the 1959 attempt on Qasim's life. Qasim barely escaped with his life, and Saddam, who was himself wounded, managed to elude the police and flee to Syria.

After spending a few months in Damascus, he moved to Egypt, where he married his cousin Sajida, with whom he would have four children. A few days after his arrival, he learned of his condemnation to death in absentia in Iraq. Not surprisingly, as he pursued his political activities and studied law at the university, he was closely watched by Nasser's police. He returned to Iraq in February 1963, as soon as Qasim was overthrown by Araf, who had taken advantage of divisions within the Ba'ath party to achieve his success. Saddam Hussein was then sent to Syria to garner Michel Aflaq's support in renewing the Ba'ath Party. Then, Hussein took a leading role in the Ba'ath Party, coordinating military activities and organizing clandestine weapons caches. When a coup attempt he had organized failed, Saddam was a wanted man again. He managed, with the help of other Ba'athists and secret messages hidden in Uday's diapers, to escape and help plot the next coup, which brought the Ba'aths to power.

Following the successful revolution of 1968, he was elected vice president of the Revolutionary Command Council, Iraq's main governing body: he was now the new regime's number two man. Among his first tasks were negotiating the 1970 treaty with the Kurds with Mustafa Barzani. He was also the main actor in reconciling Iraq with the USSR. He took over the presidency when al-Bakr retired, and held it until he was overthrown by the US in 2003.

by the war with Iran. The Iranian Revolution of 1979 put into question the application of the Algiers Agreement between the two countries, which had formalized a demarcation of the disputed border between the countries, and had in effect put an end to the Kurdish rebellion. Issues that had not been included in the pact, such as the status of three small islands in the Gulf that Iran had occupied in 1971 and the status of Khuzistan, were to come to the fore again.

Iran–Iraq War (1980–1988)

Given the very peaceful relations Iraq had enjoyed with the Shah's Iran since the Algiers Accord, it was not surprising that the Ayatollah Ruholla Khomeini (1902–1989) was suspicious of the Iraqi regime. Each side had old issues: Iraq wanted to have some control over the islands in the Gulf, and was not content to let what Iraqis called Arabistan remain the Iranian Khuzistan. Hussein's government suspected Iran of fomenting rebellion among the Iraqi Shi'ites and

Kurds; Iran accused Iraq of doing the same in Khuzistan. And the Khomeini regime made no secret of its desire to impose its concept of Shi'a Islam on all Arabs, and also to regain control over sacred Shi'a sites: Najaf and Karbala (where the two martyrs, Hussein and Hassan, were murdered), situated in Iraq. Between February 1979, a month after the fall of the Shah, and September 1980, when hostilities broke out, the Iranians multiplied provocations along the border and inside Iraq, attempting, for example, to assassinate Tariq Aziz. Ayatollah Khomeini, who had lived in Najaf for fourteen years as a political refugee, issued a call to the Iraqi people to overthrow their regime. Other Iranian leaders contributed to heighten tension in the region by openly calling for the "exportation of the Revolution." A fatwa was issued, calling for the murder of Ba'athists.

The situation was becoming tense along the frontier. In June 1979, an Iraqi air raid killed six Iranians, and such incidents took place regularly, especially during the last six months before the official beginning of the war. On September 4, 1980, Iranian artillery and aviation bombarded localities in Iraq, causing civilian deaths. For Baghdad, this date marks the beginning of the war. On September 17, Saddam broke with the Algiers Agreement. Fighting intensified and diplomatic relations broke down.

Although various border disputes—over the Gulf islands, Khuzistan/Arabistan, the Kurdish region, the Shatt al-Arab—offer an explanation for war, it seems undeniable that the timing has to do with the fact that Khomeini's Islamic revolution threatened to capture the heart of the Arab world that Saddam Hussein hoped to command for his own Ba'athist revolution. He could not tolerate the kind of opposition it seemed to be sparking within his own country, not to mention within the Arab *umma*. And he imagined, too, that post-Shah Iran had been weakened, and that a swift strike could prey on the inevitable disarray of the military following a revolution. And the Iraqi leader recognized that the United States, who wanted the Ayatollah Khomeini's revolution held in check, would be his likely ally.

Sometimes called "Saddam's Qadisiyya" in reference to the battle of 636 that opposed the Arabs and the Persians, the Iran–Iraq War raged for eight years. It ended in a ceasefire on April 20, 1988, after taking the lives of over a million Iraqi and Iranian citizens, soldiers and civilians. Even today, the demographic consequences of the war on the development of both countries remain enormous.

The Question of Kuwait

Iraq's southern border with Kuwait had long been the subject of nearly as much controversy as that with Iran. Upon the British debarkment at Fao in 1914, the British Resident in the Gulf announced that London considered the emirate of Kuwait to be "an independent state placed under British protection," and to that effect, Sir Percy Cox would draw new border lines in 1922. As long as the British remained in control of all Mesopotamia, the issue of Kuwait was deferred. But Iraqi nationalist parties never recognized the *fait accompli* of the British colonial division between Iraq and Kuwait. And nor, for that matter, did the British ever forget their intention to maintain control of the region. For example, when Faisal I, who had been placed on the throne by the British themselves, wanted to build a railroad between Baghdad and Kuwait and facilities in the port, the British refused. (Speculation exists that Faisal's mysterious death in Switzerland in September 1933 might have been linked to his longstanding desire to reestablish Iraq's historic access to Kuwait, the only deep-water port in the immediate area.)

In any case, that same year, just after the British mandate ended, Ghazi I reasserted Iraq's "inalienable right" to the emirate of Kuwait. The British promptly vetoed his trip there, where he had been invited by the new emir, Ahmed al-Sabah—in one stroke putting both rulers in their place.

In 1938, the Kuwaiti Legislative Council voted on a resolution introduced by the Movement of Free Kuwaitis, in favor of the reintegration of Kuwait into Iraq. The British replied by demanding the dissolution of the Council. Several members of the Council were arrested, and some were executed. The Free Kuwaitis' appeal to King Ghazi was rebroadcast throughout Iraq by the young king, using his own radio transmitter. This display of nationalism did not please London. The king dies in a car accident in 1939; many have testified that British intelligence arranged this.

Several times between 1930 and 1956 Iraq offered to buy or rent the deserted islands of Warbah and Budiyan belonging to Kuwait, in order to build a port there. The Kuwaitis, advised by the British, always refused. Even the construction of the port of Umm Qasr, in Iraqi territory, met with British refusal. A military base was eventually built there, but dismantled after World War II.

In Iraq, the question of Kuwait inflamed nationalist sentiment to such a point that the various pro-British governments that succeeded each other until the fall of the monarchy on July 14, 1958 never dared to officially recognize the secession. Just before the fall of the monarchy, even Nuri Said (whom nobody could accuse of being anti-British) called for the reintegration of Kuwait into the Iraqi nation.

In 1961, Great Britain abrogated the treaty it had concluded at the turn of the century with Shaykh Mubarak and the emirate became independent. Qasim immediately threatened to interrupt diplomatic relations with whatever Arab nations recognized Kuwait's new status. On June 25, Qasim declared that Kuwait was part of the vilayat of Basra, and that Iraq was going to annex it formally. He massed several battalions at the frontier. A few days later, British troops, supported by Saudi Arabia, arrived in Kuwait.

By the end of the month, Kuwait was admitted to the Arab League. Nasser had given the go-ahead, for he didn't like Qasim and feared that the new emirate would otherwise become part of the British Commonwealth. Qasim did, however, manage to obtain the Soviet Union's veto of Kuwait's candidacy for the United Nations (though it would reverse its position two years later).

Under the Iraqi regime of the Araf brothers (1963–1968), the question of the Iraq–Kuwait frontier, as drawn by British High Commissioner Perry Cox 30 years before, was again on the agenda. A common declaration was published, but not formally ratified, by the Revolutionary Command Council. The work of a task force charged with delineating the frontier was delayed, and was finally postponed indefinitely in 1967.

After the Revolution of July 1968, which brought the Ba'ath Party to power, the new regime undertook several initiatives attempting to settle the still unresolved question of Kuwait. In 1969, the Iraqi army penetrated into Kuwait to protect the port of Umm Qasr, on the Iraqi border, from a feared attack by the Shah of Iran. The troops were only withdrawn in 1977, two years after the signing of the Algiers Agreement. At this time Iraq accepted the status quo on the Kuwaiti frontier, but reiterated its demand that Kuwait sell or rent the islands of Budiyan and Warbah for Iraq to develop port facilities there.

The Iran–Iraq War only highlighted Kuwait's importance to Iraq. Strife along the Iranian border had meant that the ports of Basra and Umm Qasr were no longer in operation. The peninsula of Fao, on the Iranian side of the Shatt al-Arab, was occupied by Khomeini's troops, and so the port of Kuwait City saw a dramatic increase in activity. At the end of the war, Iraqi Foreign Minister Tariq Aziz told his Kuwaiti counterpart that he wished to reopen negotiations on the frontier, but nothing came of this overture. Iraq contends that Kuwait had taken advantage of the war to push into Iraq's territory and pump Iraqi oil.

Soon Kuwait followed American counsel to refuse the cancellation of the vast Iraqi debt incurred during the war with Iran; further, Kuwait tried to asphyxiate Iraq by pursuing a policy of dumping huge quantities of oil on the market, causing prices to plummet worldwide. Iraq, with a large population to provide for and a war-torn country to rebuild, wanted to keep oil prices high to gain revenue. The Kuwaitis (like the Saudis and others) largely invested their earning abroad, so their economic needs were actually aligned with the Western world rather than with their large Arab neighbor.

In May 1990, Saddam Hussein asked Kuwait to stop the economic war against his country to no effect. In July, Tariq Aziz sent a letter to the UN complaining that Kuwait and the United Arab Emirates were flooding the world market with a supply of oil in violation of OPEC production quotas. In what was to become a controversial meeting at the end of July, Saddam Hussein met with US Ambassador April Glaspie to discuss the conflict. The ambassador, who is on record as having said that the US had "no opinion" about Arab–Arab conflicts, like the "border disagreement with Kuwait," was immediately thereafter rather mysteriously recalled from Baghdad. The Iraqi president, in the meantime, seemed to have taken the meeting as reassurance that the US, his ally in the war against Iran, would not stand in his way this time. So it was that Saddam Hussein launched an attack on Kuwait on August 2, 1990.

The 1991 Gulf War

Such is the history that so fatally brought Iraq to Kuwait in 1990. But what of the reasons of the United States? Why, at that juncture, did the US, which had supported Iraq and the regime of Saddam Hussein throughout the Iran–Iraq War, now turn so spectacularly against the Iraqis?

Western powers, of course, had been angling for influence and power in the region at least since the decline of the Ottoman Empire. France and Great Britain had each hoped to own a lasting share in the immense wealth lying under Mosul and Kirkuk in northern Iraq. It could be said that President George Bush Sr.'s "New World Order" was simply the latest incarnation of a long line of aggressive foreign policies by Western powers in the Middle East. From the creation of Israel in 1947, to the Baghdad Pact, to the Suez Crisis, to its financial and political support of Israel, to its taking over of the British role the United States had done everything possible to consolidate power in the region. In 1991, after the fall of the USSR and after the ending of the Iran–Iraq War, the time was ripe for the US to further assert its power.

On August 6, 1990, the UN Security Council adopted Resolution 661, instituting a financial, commercial, and military boycott of Iraq. There were 13 votes for and 2 abstentions—Cuba and Yemen. The US Department of Agriculture estimated that Iraq was 75 percent dependent on foreign imports for food, and that its cereal reserves would not allow it to be self-sufficient for very long. Washington knew Saddam Hussein would be faced with a domestic disaster. Indeed, confident they had the upper hand, the United States counted on the country's collapse, and a political coup from within to eliminate Saddam Hussein's regime.

But President Bush was determined to win a war, not simply win a diplomatic or political victory. On November 29, 1990, the US pressured UN Security Council members into passing Resolution 678, authorizing

The Tragedy of the Amariya Shelter

This anti-nuclear and anti-chemical shelter, built by a Finnish company during the Iran–Iraq War to protect the inhabitants of the Baghdad neighborhood of Amariya from Iranian artillery attacks, was a target of United States bombing during the Gulf War.

On February 13, 1991, just before dawn, two penetrating bombs, "bunker-busters," pierced the reinforced concrete shell of the shelter, causing the automatic sealing of all the doors and a raging fire within the ten-foot-thick walls. The bodies of the victims were mostly scarred beyond recognition. Nevertheless, it is thought that as many as 1,200 to 1,600 people, mostly women, children, and the elderly, perished.

On the blackened walls of the bunker, like a negative from hell itself, one can make out the shadows of an old man and of a woman holding her child. On the ceiling, you can still see macabre handprints, bearing witness to the last moments of people in the upper bunks.

American authorities said that the shelter was bombed because of intelligence (allegedly emanating from Iraqi dissidents in London) that Saddam Hussein and his associates were hiding in a command post situated beneath the bunker. But that was not the case.

the use of force to remove Iraqi troops from Kuwait. And on January 16, 1991, the United States launched a massive air bombardment of Iraq and Kuwait that lasted just over a month and ended with the Iraqi withdrawal from Kuwait. Many Iraqis were killed, including soldiers who had surrendered and were retreating on the road to Basra.

According to a UNICEF report on the state of the country at the end of February, the American war had brought "instant, wide-spread economic devastation, rising poverty, the threat of impending hunger, and hardship and health setbacks." The US forces had dropped more than 88,500 tons of bombs, of which only 7 percent were actually the much-hyped "smart bombs" (statistics from Pentagon). Oil wells across the country burned for months after the 43-day war had ended. And more suffering was to come for the Iraqi people.

A Decade of Sanctions

After the end of the January war, Baghdad's partial compliance with the UN resolutions did not lead to even a partial easing of economic sanctions against Iraq. Although the lifting of the sanctions was included in UN Resolution 687, every time the easing of sanctions came on the agenda, the US came up with new demands, so much so that the sanctions continued until the 2003 US occupation of Iraq— for a total of nearly thirteen years, in what is generally acknowledged to be the most comprehensive sanctions in world history. The human toll—death, illness, malnutrition—has been extensively documented by human rights organizations. Even US officials have acknowledged the reality of the suffering, most infamously former Secretary of State Madeleine Albright, who said "We think the price is worth it" when asked if the sanctions-caused deaths of some 500,000 Iraqi children could be justified.

Denis Halliday, the UN administrator of the oil-for-food program resigned in late 1998 (after 34 years with the UN), in order to protest the impact of the sanctions on the Iraqi people (which he compares to genocide) and the oil-for-food program's inability to solve the problem. His successor, Hans von Sponeck, resigned for the same reason two years later. The oil-for-food program established in 1995

The Gulf War Syndrome

At first, there were only rumors. US soldiers who had fought in the Gulf War returned home victorious, only to find themselves plagued by a mysterious array of symptoms, including joint pain, abdominal pain and weight loss, leukemia, skin blisters, tumors, respiratory problems, decreased motor skills and concentration, and insomnia. Nearly a decade later, a report in the *American Journal of Epidemiology* (AJE) of a study of 2,000 Gulf War vets from Kansas found 34 percent of them to be suffering from classic symptoms of the so-called Gulf War illness. Extrapolating from that, as political pollsters do, means that 237,000 vets could suffer from some form of this illness.

During the Gulf War, the United States dropped nearly one million bombs that contained the Pentagon's "silver bullet." Depleted uranium (DU, or U-238). It is estimated that 200 tons of U-235 was poured on Irawi soil. DU, which is what remains when the fissionable uranium (U-234 and U-235) is removed, was hailed by military experts as a new super weapon because of its incredible density and superior penetrating power. Yet it is still radioactive, with a half-life of more than 4 billion years.

These dirty weapons have been in the making since the early days of the Cold War. When the story of sick Gulf War veterans began to surface in the early 1990s, the official Pentagon line was a denial of the connection between U-238 and any illness (as it had been with Agent Orange after Vietnam). Yet, rumbles grew within the ranks. Doug Rokke, who served as a lieutenant with the US Army Preventative Medicine Command, led teams that cleaned up vehicles contaminated by DU in the 1991 Gulf War. A doctor in a US veteran's affairs clinic admits that Rokke's own health problems are consistent with uranium exposure. Rokke contends that the US military knew of the risks, and hid them. He himself had been responsible for producing a training video teaching soldiers how to handle depleted uranium; the video was never used, and its guidelines were not followed in the 1991 war.

Then, DU was used in the war in Kosovo, and reportedly again in the 2003 war against Iraq.

This recent use is in a context in which the facts are becoming harder to deny: the European Union has devoted attention to the effects of deplete in the Kosovo conflict (about one-twentieth of that used in Iraq in 1991), longer-term studies such as the one in the *AJE* are emerging, and the World Health Organization and UNICEF both have reported enormous increases in radiation-related cancers in southern Iraq, where most of the DU fell in 1991. The population still suffers from diminished immune function; the rate of birth defects among newborns rose dramatically.

by UN Resolution 986 was to allow Iraq to sell oil in order to meet the country's humanitarian needs, but it fell seriously short of its aims, mostly because of political meddling and insufficient funds. The money from Iraq's oil sales was held in a UN-controlled account, to which Iraq had no access, and the allocation of resources was presided over by a US-dominated sanctions committee, which met in secret and was subject to the veto of any member country. Delays and shortages in the delivery of food and crucial medical supplies had devastating effects throughout the country, particarly in southern and

Iraqi Deaths Caused by the International Embargo
(1990-1997)

	Children under 5	Children over 5	Total
1990 (pre-embargo)	7 110	20 224	27 334
1990	8 903	23 561	32 464
1991	27 473	58 469	85 942
1992	46 933	76 530	123 463
1993	49 762	78 261	128 023
1994	52 906	80 776	133 682
1995	55 823	82 961	138 784
1996	56 997	83 284	140 281
1997	58 845	85 942	144 787
1998 (January to March)	17 265	22 259	39 524
Grand total	**374 907**	**592 043**	**967 950**

Source : UNESCO

The principal causes of death for children are respiratory infections, diarrhea, gastroenteritis, and malnutrition. Adult deaths are due to heart disease, hypertension, diabetes, and kidney disease.

central Iraq, whose population received disproportionately smaller allotments of oil-for-food funds than those in the Kurdish north.

The sanctions were accompanied, too, by an aerial bombardment of Iraq that was not authorized by the UN and rarely reported in the US media. And when it was, such as in a *New York Times* article headlined, "In Intense But Little-Noticed Fight, Allies Have Bombed Iraq All Year," the facts (American and British pilots firing 1,100 missiles against 359 Iraqi targets) only served to make the 2003 war seem all the more inevitable.

US-Occupied Iraq

After the terrorist attacks on New York and Washington on September 11, 2001, the second Bush administration began to escalate its attacks on Iraq. Despite the widely known reality (admitted by top State Department officials in July 2003) that there was no significant cooperation between Iraq and the al-Qaeda organization blamed for the attacks, the claim of linkage was a constant refrain. The US also continued a chorus of unsubstantiated claims that, despite the years of work by UN arms inspectors in finding and destroying 90 percent or more of Iraq's chemical, biological, and nuclear weapons programs, somehow Baghdad still represented an "imminent threat" to the US.

Washington campaigned with bribes, threats, and other pressures to win UN Security Council endorsement for a new war against Iraq. But international public opinion was strongly opposed, and the UN stood defiant. So the US, backed only by Britain, moved unilaterally to go to war.

After months of rhetoric and massing of troops, on March 19, 2003, the United States began its renewed full-scale war against Iraq. Almost immediately, Saddam Hussein's regime collapsed, and the Iraqi army put up virtually no serious resistance. Over 7,000 Iraqi civilians and an unknown number of Iraqi conscripts and other troops were killed. As the US occupation settled in, US control of Iraq's oil resources, economic rebuilding and political reconstruction was consolidated. Iraqis were denied power in their own country. However relieved Iraqis may have been at the overthrow of an oppressive regime, they did not welcome the US and British occupying forces as liberators. Instead,

small-scale guerrilla-style attacks continued, keeping US and British troops, as well as their Iraqi allies, at risk.

Within the first months following the US invasion and occupation, new information continued to surface indicating that the Bush administration's claims regarding Iraq's alleged weapons of mass destruction (WMD), its alleged efforts to buy fissile material to restore its nuclear weapons program, its alleged ties to al-Qaeda, were virtually all based on false, incomplete, exaggerated, or even forged intelligence material.

But US and British troops remain in Iraq, and the pumping of oil is beginning again.

The Human Toll

Award-winning correspondent Ed Vulliamy wrote some of the most moving coverage of the 1991 Gulf War. In 2003, he was back in Iraq to again record the devastation of war. For more of his coverage, go to **www.observer.co.uk**.

The following is excerpted from his article which appeared in the July 6, 2003 issue of The Observer:

It was Rahad's turn to hide. The nine-year-old girl found a good place to conceal herself from her playmates, the game of hide and seek having lasted some two hours along a quiet residential street in the town of Fallujah, on the banks of the Euphrates. But while Rahad crouched behind the wall of a neighbour's house, someone else—not playing the game—had spotted her, and her friends; someone above. The pilot of an American A-10 "tank-buster" aircraft, hovering in a figure of eight. He was flying an airborne weapon equipped with some of the most advanced and accurate equipment for "precision target recognition" in the Pentagon's arsenal. And at 5:30pm on 29 March, he launched his weapon at the street scene below.

The "daisy-cutter" bounced and exploded a few feet above ground, blasting red-hot shrapnel into the walls not of a tank but of houses. Rahad Septi and ten other children lost their lives; twelve were injured. Three adults were also killed.

Juma Septi, father to Rahad, holds a photograph of his daughter in the palm of his hand as he recalls the afternoon he lost his "little flower." A carpenter, Septi had been a lifelong opponent of Saddam Hussein—an activist in the Islamic Accord Party, for which he had been imprisoned, then exiled to Jordan in 1995. Last October, Septi had returned under an armistice to start a new life in his home town, reunited with his family. "I don't really know what to think now," he says. "We have lost Saddam Hussein, but I have lost my daughter."

The faithful at the door to the al-Kazimiyya sanctuary in Baghdad

── FOUR ──

Baghdad: City of Peace

"Without a doubt, of all the cities that I have visited in the East, Baghdad is the most beautiful and the most important, to my mind. It is an oasis in the middle of the surrounding desert, a queen born of the desert peoples that traversed her land, and finally, the capital of a powerful empire of the future."

—*Count Laurent de Sercey (1840)*

The glorious Baghdad of the Arab Golden Age is hidden by the crisis of the last decade. *Madinat al-Salam*, the city of peace, was the dream of Caliph Abu Jaffar al-Mansur, who founded the city in the 8th century. Few cities have been as coveted and as brutalized as Baghdad. An impressive number of plots, betrayals, and massacres have taken place within its walls. From a peak of over 2 million inhabitants during the time of Harun al-Rashid, the city's population had dwindled by the start of the 20th century to about 180,000 people, after centuries of massacres, civil wars, floods, enduring poverty, and the repeated epidemics of the 19th century.

Baghdad owes its existence today to the incredible energy of its people. Mesopotamia has always absorbed great conquerors, and treated its wounds on its own. Even after the 1991 Gulf War and during the decade of sanctions, building projects were still visible in Baghdad. Schools, caravanserais, sanctuaries, monuments, bridges, and official buildings were somehow being maintained and in some cases restored. There are more vestiges of Baghdad's glorious past than one would think, and more legends about the city than in the *Thousand and One Nights*.

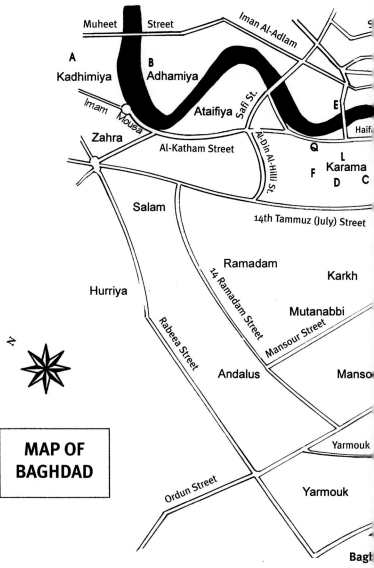

MAP OF BAGHDAD

Main Hotels and Restaurants
1. Hotel Al-Mansour
2. Hotel Rachid
3. Hotel Novotel Al Sadeer
4. Hotel Babylon
5. Hotel Bagdad
6. Hotel Ishtar Sheraton
7. Hotel Palestine Meridien
8. Restaurant Khan Marjan

Sites of Interest
A. Sanctuary of Khadimiyya
B. Imam al-Adham Mosque
C. Mausoleum of al-Hallaj (cenotaph)
D. Shaykh Marouf Mosque
E. Abbasid Palace
F. "Tomb of Zubayda"
G. Wastani Gate
H. Shaykh Omar Mosque

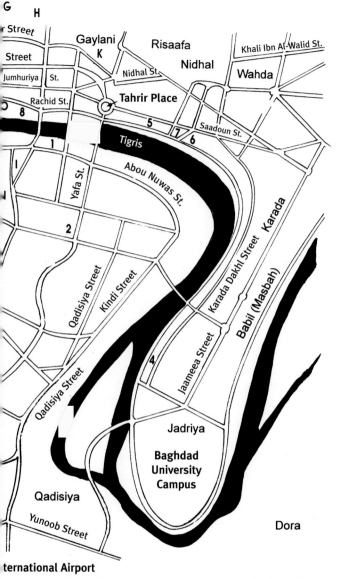

G H

Street

Gaylani
Street K

Risaafa

Khali Ibn Al-Walid St.

Nidhal

Jumhuriya St.

Nidhal St.

Wahda

Rachid St.

Tahrir Place

8

5 7 6

Saadoun St.

Tigris

1

Abou Nuwas St.

Yafa St.

2

Karada Dakhl Street

Karada

Babil (Masbah)

Qadisiya Street

Kindi Street

Jaameea Street

4

Jadriya

Qadisiya Street

Baghdad
University
Campus

Qadisiya

Yunoob Street

Dora

ternational Airport

I. National Museum
J. International Fairgrounds
K. Shaykh Abdul Qadar al-Ghailani Mosque
L. Junayd's Tomb
M. Khulafa Mosque
N. Train Station
O. Copperware market (Safafir Souk)/ Khan Marjan
Caravanserai/ al-Mustansiriya/ al-Asafiya Mosque
(same area)

P. National Folklore Museum
Q. Saddam Hussein Modern Art Museum

The National Museum

*Clockwise, from left: Statue of Salmanasar II (Assyria), Statue of Hercules (Hatra),
Miniature temple in marble (Hatra)*

Baghdad's Beginnings

In the second millenium before Christ, the city of Shaduppum (Tell Harmal) flourished a mere five miles from present-day Baghdad: this is how long human beings have found sustenance on this spot of earth.

Some scholars think that Baghdad is an Aramaic name, a deformation of the words *Beyt* and *Kadad*, or "sheep corral." Others have asserted that Persians built the original village of Baghdad, for in Farsi, *Bagh* means god, and Baghdad, "gift of god."

In any case, we know that the name Baghdad was not used in Persia until the 8th century BCE, although the city had been in existence since Mesopotamian antiquity: it is mentioned in a legal tablet dating from the time of Hammurabi (1800 BCE). The city did not vanish afterward; a stone marking the city limits, with the inscription "Baghdadi" was found proving the city's survival through the reign of the Kassite king Mazimarut (1341–1316 BCE). Another stone marker from the time of the Babylonian king, Marduk Apalidin (1208–1195) refers to the city as "Baghdadu."

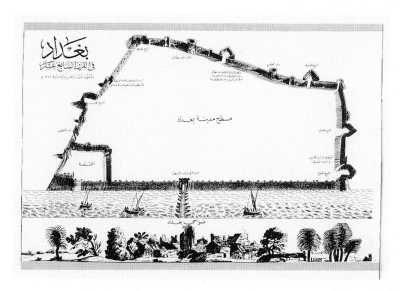

17th-century map of the ancient city drawn by Jean-Baptiste Tavernier

The present-day neighborhood of al-Karkh, a famous market in Abbasid times, became a fortified village on the west bank of the Tigris during the reign of Shapur II (309–379).

When Caliph al-Mansur arrived on the scene, in search of a site for his new city that would be easy to defend and boast a good climate, there was a monastery, Dayr al-Atiq, and a few tiny villages peopled by Nestorian Christians, descendants of Byzantine slaves or prisoners. The Caliph was received by monks who told him that an old legend had prophesied that a magnificent city would one day stand there. With Mansur's donation to the monastery, the Nestorians were easily convinced to give the Caliph their blessing to build his city. A French traveller who visited Baghdad in the 17th century, Jean-Baptiste Tavernier, recounts that, 50 years before he arrived, the tomb of a bishop and some of the monks' cells had been unearthed right in the middle of the city, during the construction of a caravanserai. Those ruins might well have been the remains of the ancient al-Atiq monastery.

The location of Baghdad was, as the Caliph had wished, strategic: on the road to both the Mediterranean and Anatolia from Persia, and fed by a powerful river. Caliph al-Mansur had his astrologer verify the auspiciousness of the site, then set about recruiting 100,000 workers, including the best architects and artisans of the Islamic world. Work began in 762, in spite of rumors spread by the inhabitants of the nearby city of Kufa, jealous not to have been chosen, about water from the Tigris making horses deaf and men impotent. Construction of Mansur's capital took four years; the Caliph named the new city Madinat al-Salam, which is one of the names of Paradise in the Qur'an. Some historians would later assert that Baghdad was situated on the exact site of the Garden of Eden.

The city was circular, like a nomad encampment, with a layout similar to those of Uruk and Hatra. A double wall some 30 yards high protected it, with towers placed at regular intervals and a circular moat ringing the wall. Four gates were situated at equal distance from each other, a little over a mile apart; they were named after the cities to which the road from each *bab*, or gate, led: Basra, Khorassan,

Damascus, and Kufa. These were doubled by the gates of the inner wall, built out of bricks and a mortar made of bitumen. On the upper level, called a *majlis*, a gallery ran the length of the crenellated wall. It was wide enough for the Caliph to ride on horseback and observe the surrounding country. As in the city of Hatra, one entered Baghdad by a road that ran along the outer wall, which enabled guards to inspect arrivals at leisure, and safely fire upon approaching enemies. The wall passed near the current site of Shaykh Marouf's tomb, in a cemetery behind Baghdad Station.

The residential zone was divided into sections where the officers and partisans of the Caliph had their quarters, each according to the area where his clan originated, with gated walls dividing the sections of the city. The inhabited zone of the ancient city extended in a semi-circle around the Caliph's palace, which was also surrounded by a wall.

Al-Mansur's Palace, nicknamed the Golden Gate for its heavily gilded great door, stood in the middle of Baghdad. Made of marble and stone, it boasted a magnificent green dome over fifty yards high topped by a statue of a mounted warrior. A mosque with its minaret was annexed to the palace. Some of the stones that went into the construction of the complex came from Chosroes' ruined palace at Ctesiphon.

Baghdad soon became the greatest commercial city of its time. Specialized markets were installed in arcades along four streets radiating from the center of the city. These markets were soon transferred to al-Karkh for reasons of safety. Later on, some would be set up outside the city limits, with the foreign merchants in a separate zone. Interestingly, Iraqi merchants sometimes paid by check, a practice already widespread in the Gulf region and in India.

Baghdad developed rapidly. In 775, al-Mansur had built a new palace, called Qasr al-Khuld (the Castle of Eternity), another of the names of the Qur'anic Paradise. He also built a military garrison on the left bank of the Tigris, placing it under the command of his son and heir, al-Mahd. This area of Baghdad would later be called al-Rusafa, from the name of a palace built there by Harun al-Rashid.

There is no longer any trace left of the round city. Lightning destroyed the green dome. Referring to the war of succession that broke out after the death of Harun al-Rashid, the 9th-century Persian scholar al-Tabari wrote that "destruction and ruin rained down upon Baghdad until there was nothing left of its splendor." The Castle of Eternity disappeared in the 12th century.

Baghdad would be reborn bigger and more beautiful after al-Mamun's 813 victory over his brother, the Caliph al-Amin. Although after 836 it was eclipsed by Samara, just 62 miles (100 km) upstream on the Tigris, Baghdad came back into prominence. Caliph al-Mutahid (892–902) had several palaces built, including the famous Palace of the Tree. Al-Mutahid possessed an extraordinary contraption: a tree with birds sculpted of precious metals that moved and sang thanks to a mechanism inside the gold and silver trunk.

Baghdad survived far beyond the prediction of the Persian astrologer Nawbaht, who linked the life span of the city to the number 309, based on a sura in the Qur'an.

MOSQUES AND MUSLIM SANCTUARIES

Abu Hanifa Mosque

This mosque is situated in the Azamiya quarter (named for Hanifa, who was also known as "al-Imam al-Azam," or the greatest of imams.

Ibn Thabet al-Kufa, otherwise known as Abu Hanifa ("the one who carries the inkwell") had a Persian grandfather. He was born in Kufa in 700. He grew up to be both a silk merchant and a teacher of religion. His lectures on Islamic law and morals were followed by a number of disciples. He founded a school of jurists whose precepts were later made official and applied in the entire Ottoman Empire. Today, the Hanafite rite is the most common in Islam, and remains the form of Islam that is closest to what it was in Mohammad the Prophet's day.

Abu Hanifa died in prison in Baghdad in 767, accused of sedition and refusing the charge of Qadi (supreme religious judge) that Caliph al-Mansur offered him. He was buried on the grounds of his school, and a cemetery called al-Khaizuran eventually grew around his tomb.

A sanctuary was erected on Abu Hanifa's tomb in 1066 under the

Seljuk Turks, but Shah Abbas destroyed it during the Persian occupation of Iraq. The current mosque dates from the Ottoman Sultan, Murad IV (1638). It was restored in 1802 by Sulaiman Pasha. The imam's remains rest in a tomb encircled by a silver fence.

Shaykh Abdelkader al-Ghailani Mosque

The al-Ghailani Mosque was erected on the site of the school where the shaykh taught, and where he was buried in 1166.

Called the "Supreme Savior" by his disciples, Abdelkader al-Ghailani is one of the great saints of Sunni Islam. Both his father and mother were members of Imam Ali's clan. He was born in 1077 in the region of Ghailan, on the southern coast of the Caspian Sea, though some say he was born in Guil, a village situated between Baghdad and Wasit. A powerful theologian and charismatic preacher, he converted many Christians and Jews. Legends about him abound, including one in which he comes back from the dead to help his disciples in their spiritual quest.

The *tariqa qadriya* (religious brotherhood), which dispenses al-Ghailani's teachings is chronologically the first, and still one of the foremost, of the Sufi orders of Islam: its influence extends to Africa and Asia. Emir Abdelkader, who opposed the French conquest of Algeria, was one of its North African members.

The mosque was destroyed by the Mongols, then destroyed again by the Persians, who expelled the al-Ghailani family from Baghdad.

Sulaiman the Magnificent embellished the mosque with a dome in 1535, an achievement of great architectural beauty. The Ottoman ruler gave the al-Ghailani clan the title of *naquib al-ashraf*, signifying recognition of their descendence from the Prophet, and conferring special privileges upon the clan.

Around the courtyard of the mosque, rooms are reserved for pilgrims from the four corners of the Islamic world. A well-furnished library serves religious students and researchers, with its precious ancient copies of the Qur'an and other manuscripts with superb calligraphy and illumination.

The monument again fell into the hands of the Persians in 1623 and was desecrated. When Sultan Murad IV took Baghdad in 1638, he restored the edifice, and had a fence of pure silver installed around the mausoleum of the Supreme Savior.

Abdurahman al-Ghailani, Shaykh of the *qadriya* in the 1920s, who presided the first Iraqi Ministerial Council, is interred under a pillar of the mosque. He had a clock built for the sanctuary by artisans from Bombay. The two sons of Abdelkader, who succeeded him as directors of the school, are interred in the open courtyards.

Since the time of Sulaiman the Magnificent, the mosque has had an *imaret* (a soup kitchen). It distributes about 1,200 free meals a day to the needy.

Shaykh Marouf's Mosque

Shaykh Marouf al-Karkhi, known as the Protector of Baghdad, was originally a Sabean or Christian from the Wasit region. He converted to Islam, and ever since his death in 815 has been revered as one of the great Sufi masters.

His mausoleum stands in the midst of an old cemetery named after him, which was renovated in the 1990s.

Shaykh Omar Mosque

Omar Suhrawardi (died 1234) was the author of one of the best-known orthodox Sufi treatises. He is said to be a descendant of Caliph Abu Bakr, and was called the "Shaykh of Shaykhs."

Shaykh Omar taught the Shafeite form of Islam, with a judicial system based Mohammed el-Shafei's early 9th-century interpretations of the Qur'an, the *hadiths* (Prophet Mohammad's commentaries), and *sunna* (Islamic tradition). Shaykh Omar was the Sufis' primary representative at the court of al-Nasir (1180–1225). This Caliph, whose ambition was to unite the different currents of Islam, found an influential partisan in this Sufi mystic.

Shaykh Omar's 13th-century Seljuk-style mausoleum, with its honey-combed dome, is visible from afar. The mosque was actually built in 1511.

The sanctuary is situated near the central gate of Baghdad (Bab al-Wastani). Today, the ring road that follows the trace of the ancient wall runs past the small graveyard on its way to the Gate of the Talisman.

The Tomb of Zumurud Khatum, or the Tomb of Zubayda

In Shaykh Marouf's cemetery, behind the train station and near the railroad tracks, there is a monumental tomb, topped with a conical dome shaped like a beehive. For a long time, people thought it was the tomb of Zubayda, the wife of Caliph Harun al-Rashid, who died in 831, or of a forgotten princess who shared the same first name and whom popular memory had ended up confusing with the famous caliph's wife. In fact, it is the tomb of Zumurud (Emerald) Khatun, mother of Caliph al-Nasir, and was built in 1202. Zubayda is actually interred in the Qoresh cemetery, where today the al-Kazimiyya mosque now stands.

The octagonal façade of the building is decorated with geometric designs. Inside a square room the simple catafalque is covered with a green cloth. Egg-shaped holes in the dome provide natural lighting. The white walls are browned from countless handprints in henna left by pilgrims as tokens of their requests to the saint.

The Tomb of Joshua

The Mausoleum is located at the entrance to Shaykh Marouf's cemetery, near the Baghdad train station.

During the reign of Caliph al-Amin, Harun's elder son, the Tigris flooded, and uncovered an apparently very ancient tomb. A commission made up of Muslim, Christian, and Jewish clerics decreed that the tomb was that of the Patriarch Joshua (Nabi Yushua), whose remains had been transported to Iraq during the first exodus of the Jews. The Caliph had the tomb covered by a mausoleum.

According to Denis de Rivoyre, a French traveller who visited Baghdad in 1880, the Joshua interred there was a Jewish rabbi. Actually, the tomb was disputed between Jews and Muslims for centuries, with the former apparently having won out, for the tomb was converted to a synagogue. But in 1885, Sultan Abdul Hamid decided in favor of the Muslims, and Joshua's tomb became a mosque. When the British took over, they dared not reverse this decision, for fear of provoking religious riots.

A remarkable fact about this site is that at night, it is guarded by a snake. During the day, the reptile lives in the cool cavities of the excavation under the mausoleum, and hibernates during winter. Another snake is currently being trained to take over when the current guard dies. The human guard has traditionally been from the same family that was given the charge long ago. It is said that this family has kept alive the knowledge of the medicinal plants that are grown in a garden near the mausoleum.

The Iraqi Ministry of Religious Affairs has ordered extensive digs to be conducted there by Iraqi archaeologists, to see if the true identity of the tomb's original occupant can be scientifically determined.

Baba Guru Nanak's Cenotaph, Tombs of al-Bahlul and Junayd

The tomb of Joshua is right next to that of Guru Nanak (1469–1538), founder of the Sikh religion. His cenotaph is an important destination for Sikh pilgrims, most of whom come from India and Pakistan. Wahb Ibn Omar al-Kufi, also known as al-Bahlul (the Crazy One), is buried in a room nearby. This great Sufi, a cousin of Caliph Harun al-Rashid, feigned insanity in order not to fulfill any official function, even an honorific one.

Shaykh Junayd al-Bagdadi, a late-9th-century Sufi master, is buried nearby. Once known as "the Lord of those who know Allah," he had great influence on the thought of al-Hallaj (see page 79). Al-Hallaj, however, ended up excluding the mystic from his entourage, having had enough of his extravagant behavior. Indeed, he considered Junayd truly insane.

Ahmadiya Mosque

The Ahmadiya Mosque dates from the late 18th century. It is a mix of the Persian and Turkish architectural styles, and possesses a beautiful *minbar* made of Mosul marble, and decorated in flower-motif tiles.

It is situated on the Midan, a large square that served as marketplace and parading grounds.

Al-Khulafa Mosque

The Caliph's Mosque (al-Khulafa) is more often called al-Ghazal, after the minaret of al-Ghazal Souk (wool market).

The recently built edifice replaced a 19th-century Ottoman mosque;

its minaret dates from the 10th century. It was part of the mosque of the Caliph's palace, built after the transfer of the capital from Samara to Baghdad, long ago. The mosque was destroyed during the Mongol invasion, but rebuilt in 1279 by Abaqa, Hulagu's son.

With its inscription in Kufic style on a band with intricate moldings, and an ornate balcony supported by an assemblage of stalactites, its minaret resembles the one in the village of Kiffle, near Ezekial's tomb.

Sayyid Sultan Ali Mosque

Built in 1860 and restored by Sultan Abdul Hamid forty years later, this mosque honors Sayyid Sultan Ali, one of the founders of the Rifai brotherhood. He was particularly revered by the Ottoman soldiers stationed in Iraq.

Al-Khulani Mosque

Situated on al-Khulani Square, in front of the Ministry of Trade, this mosque is unique in that its dome is higher than its minaret.

Al-Kazimiyya Sanctuary

This sanctuary honoring "the two Kazims," is one of the most sacred places for Shi'a Muslims. It gets its name from the seventh and the ninth of the twelve imams: Mussa al-Kazim and his grandson, Mohammed al-Taqi. This religious edifice is in the process of being restored and modernized.

Mussa al-Kazim was the son of Jafar al-Sadiq, the Sixth Imam, who was poisoned in 765 by Caliph al-Mansur. His son Ismail, whom he had designated as his heir, had died before him, or been "hidden," resulting in a serious conflict of succession and the second schism within the Shi'a faith. According to some accounts, Mussa's and Ismail's father, an imam who studied esoteric sciences and was the author of a treatise on divination, knew that Ismail would die prematurely, and also that he would come back before the end of time to reveal the hidden meaning of the Qur'an. The partisans of Ismail were called Ismailis or Septimal Shi'ites. Accused of heresy, they were forced underground.

For others, Ismail had not deserved his father's trust; they doubted

The Casnazaniyya Dervishes

Not far from a place called Nafaq al-Shorta (Policemen's Tunnel) is a religious center (*takyah*) of the Casnazaniyya *tariqa*, one of the principal Sufi brotherhoods. Every Monday and Thursday, mystic ceremony is held there.

After evening prayers, which take place inside in winter and in the courtyard in summer, the dervishes, surrounded by numerous faithful and curious onlookers, chant the 99 names of Allah and extracts from the Qur'an while swaying from side to side. Tambourines accompany the chant, which, after about an hour, takes the sufis into a trance.

Shaykh Mohammad al-Casnazani, head of the brotherhood, prays with his disciples. When he feels the time has come, he goes and sits down at the entrance of the *takyah*. A great rug is unrolled in front of him. A *maqam* singer, surrounded by tambourine players, intones religious chants, then the dervishes arrive, and begin their favorite exercises: keeping a flaming torch inside their mouths, or chewing and swallowing razor blades, glass, cutting their tongues with knives, sticking daggers in their heads, or piercing their livers or their tongues with needles. No signs of suffering appear on the faces of these mystics, nor hemorrhage or inflammation; their wounds heal rapidly.

The dervishes assert that Allah has granted the Sufi masters the power to perform *caramat* (miracles) to help them spread Islam. The physical tortures they inflict upon themselves are a proof of their spiritual strength.

The Casnazani are Arabs who took refuge in Kurdistan, in the Sulaimaniya region, to escape religious persecution. The Casnazani brotherhood gets its name from Abdul Karim Shah al-Casnazani, who died in 1889. This man, known for his great religious devotion, once spent two years praying in a cave in Kurdistan. Upon his return, his uncle, appointed him Shaykh of the brotherhood.

Headquartered in Carabejna, in Kurdistan, the brotherhood developed rapidly. The Casnazani got their prestige from the *caramat* that they regularly accomplish, notably through the healing of incurable diseases and, somewhat more prosaically, for having fought the British during World War I. Carabejna was firebombed by the Royal Air Force.

his morals and accused him of drunkenness. They assert that before his death, Jafar told Mussa, Ismail's half-brother, that he would be the next Imam. Mussa al-Kazim (the Silent One, or the One Who Hides), the Seventh Imam, had five successors. His partisans, after the chain of succession had ended, became known as the Ithna'asharis (literally, Twelvers). By the 15th century, this sect, with its allegiance to twelve imams, had emerged as the predominant one.

It has been said that Mussa al-Kazim was poisoned by Harun al-Rashid in 818. The Caliph was obliged to show the body of the dead imam to prove that he had not been a victim of foul play, and that the imam had died a natural death.

His grandson, Mohammed al-Taqi (the Pious), the Ninth Imam, was buried later near al-Kazim. He had succeeded Ali al-Rida, who was poisoned by Caliph al-Ma'mun. After the assassination of al-Rida, the caliph, to patch things up with the Shi'ites, invited Mohammed al-Taqi to Baghdad and offered him his daughter's hand. This imam died in 835, poisoned by Caliph al-Mu'tassim.

A mausoleum was erected by the Buwayhid sultan, Mu'iz al-Dawla, in 947. It was burned by the Mongols in 1258, then rebuilt at the beginning of the 16th century by Shah Ismail, who claimed descendence from Imam Mussa.

The sanctuary was finished by Sulaiman the Magnificent, and renovated several times since. The two domes, placed above the tombs of the imams, are flanked by four minarets and covered in gold leaf. The great entrance gate is richly decorated.

A vast courtyard surrounds the sanctuary and is enclosed by a wall covered with tiles decorated with Qur'anic verses. There are also guestrooms for pilgrims.

CHRISTIAN CHURCHES

Roman Catholic Church

Near the al-Chorja souk, on Caliphs' Street, this 1866 church is situated on a site where once stood a church devoted to Saint Thomas. Laid out in the shape of a cross, this church boasts a dome 35 yards high.

The tomb of a famous Iraqi linguist, Father Aristias Marie al-Karmali, is situated inside.

Orthodox Armenian Church
This church on Midan Square is also called Church of the Virgin Mary, and sometimes Church of Miskinta, from the name of a 5th-century martyr. It has a supposedly magical chain that attracts many visitors, who wrap the chain around their head while making a wish.

Armenian Catholic Church
This church, near al-Ghazal souk, on Caliphs' Street, is also called the Church of the Assumption. It was last restored in 1883.

Chaldean Church (University Street)
This University Street church is known as both St. Mary's Church and the Church of the Virgin Sultana al-Wardia. It was built in 1898.

The Armenian Catholic Church

Syriac Church

This church on Kharrada al-Sharqiyya Street, built in 1969, is the newest of the churches listed.

ANCIENT MONUMENTS

Al-Mustansiriya Madrasa and Surroundings

This school (madrasa) was built in 1234 under the reign of the Seljuk Turks, by the next-to-last Abbasid Caliph, al-Mustansir Billah. It is considered among the first universities of the world. Ibn Batuta, the great Moroccan traveller who visited the university in the early 14th century, during the reign of the Sultan Abu Said (1316–1335), recounts that "the school represents the four orthodox rites, with each possessing its own section, a mosque and a classroom. The lessons take place under a small wooden dome, and the teacher is seated on a chair covered with a rug. He is grave, dressed in black, with a turban. At his right and left are two assistants, who repeat everything that he says. This is the manner in which all four rites hold their assemblies. Inside the school there is a bath for the students, and a chamber for holy ablutions."

Al-Mustansiriyya, situated on the left bank of the Tigris, near the Bridge of Shuwadas (Martyrs), has by miracle escaped floods and destruction. At the start of the last century, it was practically in ruins, after having been used as a caravanserai, then occupied by customs officials. It has been since restored, but cracks appeared in the building during the Gulf War bombings. And unfortunately, on April 2, 2003, American bombs directly hit the university.

In the entrance, there was once a famous clock that indicated the position of the sun and the moon each hour, but it has not been reconstructed. The inner courtyard is bracketed by two *iwans*, semi-circular vaults that open onto the courtyard and are reserved for the study of the Qur'an and hadiths.

Situated just behind the north *iwan*, the Asafiya Mosque used to belong to a monastery of whirling dervishes built during the 17th century by vizier Sinan Pasha Jighalzadeh, a Christian converted to Islam after Ottoman pirates took him and his father prisoner. The mosque and its minaret date from the 19th century.

Al-Mustansiriya madrasa: at center, one of the two iwans. *In the background, the al-Asafiya minaret.*

Alongside the madrasa, on the Tigris near the souk, stands the al-Khaffafin Mosque. It was built by Zumurud Khatum, mother of the Caliph al-Nasir. There is a traditional café, where men smoke narghilahs, on the corner.

The Funeral Mosque of Qadi Abdallah al-Aquli (1240–1327), one of the best-known students of al-Mustansiriya, is situated about 400 yards down the street, on the other side of Rashid Street. Al-Aquli was an eminent jurist whose decisions in legal and religious matters made a great contribution to Islamic jurisprudence. The building dates from the 14th century, with restorations from two centuries later.

Palace of the Abbasids

Discovered in 1900 near the left bank of the Tigris, the ruins of the ancient palace were thought at first to be from the Abbasid epoch,

The Passion of al-Hallaj

The cenotaph of al-Hallaj (the Keeper of Consciences), a Muslim mystic executed for heresy in the 9th century, is one of the least known religious sites of Baghdad. It is an obligatory stop for those who know the life and poems of the martyr. The famous French orientalist Louis Massignon experienced a spiritual awakening through his study of al-Hallaj's life and works.

Located a few hundred yards from the old cemetery of Baghdad, on a dead-end street lined with houses said to be reserved for widows, the sanctuary is kept by a blind elderly man who receives visitors with solemnity, dressed in a long tunic called a *abaya*.

Born in Persia in 858, al-Hallaj moved to Iraq when he was young. He knew the Qur'an by heart by the age of twelve, and had already taken to ascetic habits. During his first pilgrimage to Mecca, he is said to have fasted for a year in total silence next to the Qa'aba.

The inflamed sermons the ascetic imam pronounced in Iran, then in India and in Turkistan, attracted many followers, but also many enemies. In Baghdad, he called upon Muslims to "save him from Allah" and told them, "Allah has made my blood lawful for you: kill me!" He was accused of being a fake, or worse, a Karmat agent, sent by those who stole the Qa'aba. Some said he should be condemned to death. Suspected of plotting to overthrow the established order, al-Hallaj fled to Persia, but in 911, he was arrested, and spent nine years imprisoned in Baghdad. Caliph al-Muktadir provided discrete support out of gratitude for al-Hallaj's having treated him once, but could not prevent his ultimate trial and execution.

Al-Hallaj died on March 27, 922 in horrible conditions. A huge crowd noted his last words. He was then dismembered and decapitated. His body was burned and his ashes thrown into the Tigris. His followers gathered some of his ashes and gave them a proper burial. Many Sunni Muslims, especially in India, consider him to be a saint.

during the rule of Caliph al-Ma'mun (813–833). Later, it was thought to be a building called Dar al-Musanat, erected during the reign of Caliph al-Nasir (1180–1225).

In 1946, the Iraqi scholar Ma'aruf claimed that the palace was the al-Sharabiya madrasa, founded in 1231 by Sharaf al-Din al-Sharabi. If this is true, that would mean the building dates from the reign of al-Mustansir. This madrasa was the educational organ of the Hanbalite sect of Islam (founded by al-Hanbal, 780–855).

Its *iwan* is similar to that of the nearby Mustansiriya madrasa. Renovations begun in 1935 have not yet been finished, but in recent years a parallel *iwan* has been added. Upper stories with rooms for students have been rebuilt, which give out onto raised galleries around the central courtyard.

Bab al-Wastani

The wall built on the left bank of the Tigris, in al-Rusafa quarter, dates from Caliph al-Mustarshid Billah (1118–1135). It was still standing at the end of the 19th century. The ramparts were of semi-circular form, beginning near the level of the Tigris, near the Sabata'sh Tammuz (July 17th) Bridge, and stretches to the Jumhuriya (Republican) Bridge. The wall had four gates, as follows:

Bab al-Sultan, later called Bab al-Mu'adham, which was demolished during the construction of Rashid Street;

Bab al-Dhafariya, also called al-Kazpu, the White Gate, then Bab al-Wastani, the Middle Gate, which was rebuilt at the beginning of the 13th century. It has been restored and is now a museum;

Bab al-Halaba, later called Bab al-Tillisim, or the Gate of the Talisman. This name was given in reference to the sculpture that decorated the gate from the time of Caliph al-Nasir (circa 1230), of a person seated between two formidable open-mouthed dragons. The Ottoman Sultan Murad IV had the gate walled after retaking Baghdad in 1638. The Turks then used it as an arms depot, and blew it up in 1917. It is not known whether they wished to destroy this symbol of Ottoman power, or simply prevent the British from gaining access to the weapons stored there.

Bab al-Wastani

Bab al-Basiliya, later called Bab al-Sharki, was demolished in 1937 in order to extend Rashid Street. It was situated where al-Tahrir Square now stands.

A new gate, the Mosul, in the north of Baghdad, was built recently (1983), but pays tribute to the Abbasid dynasty, with fifteen-yard-high arches decorated with mosaics.

Al-Kushela

This building has a Turkish name, meaning "garrison." Indeed, the guard of the Pasha was quartered there, in a building connected to the *serai* (palace) through the inner courtyard. A marble tower, 75 feet high and topped with a clock and a weathervane, was built by Mahdat Pasha in 1868 to wake up his soldiers.

Marjaniya Madrasa

Built in 1357 by Amin ad-Din Marjan, the governor of Baghdad under the Jalarid Dynasty, this Muslim religious school dispensed theological instruction, following the Hanafite and Shafeite rites. The school received income from several commercial buildings attached to it, including a caravanserai, the Khan Marjan (see adjacent page).

In 1785, Sulaiman Pasha, governor of Baghdad, transformed the madrasa into a mosque. In 1871, Midhat Pasha had its walls plastered over during the Shah of Persia's visit to Iraq.

In 1944, the municipality of Baghdad had begun to demolish the madrasa, intending to replace it with an open square. The foremen of the site spotted ornamental inscriptions in the foundations and notified the Directorate of Antiquities, which immediately stopped the excavations. The inscriptions on brick from the *musala* (prayer room) are now on display in the Baghdad Museum.

Serai

This Turkish word designates the residence of the Pasha under the Ottomans. The Baghdad serai is located on the left bank of the Tigris.

It was pillaged under Dawud Pasha in the early 19th century, and left abandoned until 1850, when a new governor decided to restore it.

The massacre of the Janissaries, then of the Mameluks, as well as the coronation of Faisal I all took place in the courtyard of the serai.

Khan Marjan Caravanserai

Khans, or caravanserais, were inns for caravans and travellers that dotted the various trade routes in the Middle East and Asia. Baghdad possessed several.

The Khan Marjan, or Khan Ortamah, was built in 1358 by Amin al-Din Marjan in the quarter of the al-Thalatha Souk (Tuesday Market). Its inner vault is 50 feet high. Rooms for travellers and merchants were situated on the upper floors.

The Khan is now a restaurant after having served as a museum, and as a warehouse for buttons.

Khan Marjan

MUSEUMS

The National Museum

The first Iraqi museum was founded in 1923 in the Serai gallery, then the collections were transported to a new site as the volume of archeological finds increased. This museum, inaugurated in 1966, is the work of a German architect.

A huge expository space, the museum also houses a library and an auditorium. The galleries, devoted to Iraq's different historical periods, follow chronological order: prehistory, Sumer, Babylon, Akkad, the Kassites, the Assyrians, Chaldeans and Achemenids, Hatrana and Parthians, Sassanids and Muslims. Two rooms are devoted to coinage and ivory.

The National Museum was very much in the news in the aftermath of the 2003 American bombing of Baghdad. Archeologists and art

Selling spices in al-Chorja Souk

historians from around the world had been concerned throughout the build-up to the war about the protection of the incredible treasures of this museum—the gold treasures of Nimrud, the Uruk vase, the Lady of Uruk, the Harmal lions, the gold lyre of Ur, to name but a few—and indeed, most important items that could be moved before the war were. In the looting and destruction that followed the fall of Baghdad, an international panic arose about the loss of much of the museum's collection. As the dust settled, some of the most prized items in the museum (such as Nimrud's gold) were found to be safe in a secret, flooded, vault in the country's Central Bank. Still, at latest count, nearly 50 of the most important pieces of the collection and many lesser items (though lesser is a relative term, in this ancient land!) are still missing. Years of work are ahead, by any estimate, to restore the museum and its collection to a place where people can visit and learn from the work of past civilizations.

Baghdad Museum

In this museum on Mamun Street, scenes from daily life, traditional crafts, and Baghdad culture are represented through photos, paintings, and models. The museum owns a well-stocked library specializing in the history of the city. On Fridays, music lovers can hear *maqam* concerts, with the best musicians and singers of the country.

Dar Saddam

Located in the Haifa quarter, in a traditional house that was saved from destruction, this museum possesses over 40,000 ancient manuscripts. In one section, there is a census of privately owned collections, boasting admirably illuminated manuscripts from the first centuries of Islam.

The House of Fashion

Founded in 1979, this museum recreates costumes of the various epochs of Iraq's long history. The House of Fashion regularly organizes sumptuous shows in Baghdad and abroad.

Museum of Iraqi Art Pioneers

Contains works by painters of the Iraqi modern art movement (pre-1949).

Saddam Modern Art Museum

Works of contemporary Iraqi painters.

War Museum

Collections of ancient weapons, and the history of the Iraqi Army since its foundation.

BAGHDAD LANDMARKS

Rashid Street

Rashid Street used to be Baghdad's main street. First called Khalil Pasha Street, from the name of the Turkish governor of the city who had it built in 1897, it was meant to facilitate the movement of soldiers. Under the British Mandate, it was called New Street, then al-Rashid Street, in homage to the caliph of the *Thousand and One Nights*. Since the 1970s, Rashid Street has lost in popularity to Saadun Street.

During the pro-British monarchy, the numerous cafés and restaurants on Rashid Street were the preferred meeting-places of Baghdad's intellectuals and nationalists. There is a statue commemorating the attempt against General Qasim's life, in which Saddam Hussein was a key participant.

With its shaded arcades and boutiques, Rashid Street is one of the liveliest of the city, and one of the more pleasant during the hot days of summer. On the small streets that branch out toward the Tigris, souks sell traditional goods such as silver jewelry, copperware, and rugs.

As late as the end of the century, the Hussein Ajemi Café, otherwise known as the Poets' Café, between Mutanabi Street and al-Haraj Souk, still attracted Baghdad's many poetry lovers on Fridays. In the early 20th century, Iraq's great poets, al-Zahawi and al-Rusafi, had held their literary jousts here. A statue of the former stands at the intersection leading toward the Mustansiriya madrasa.

Rashid Street in the 1940s

A bit further down the arcade, going toward Midan Square, one can taste the best *zibib* (a drink made from macerated raisins) in Baghdad at chez Haj Zubala, or relax at the Umm Kulthum Café, to the ethereal sound of the famous Egyptian singer's beautiful voice, which plays all day over the loudspeaker. The walls of the place are a veritable photographic museum of Umm Kulthum's life.

Rashid Street gives out onto the Bab al-Sharqi. In the 1970s still stood the famous hotel, Tigris Palace, where Agatha Christie often stayed while in Iraq with her husband, an archaeologist. She wrote three detective novels about Mesopotamia there.

The First Cafés of Baghdad

Cafés have long had a special place in the daily life of Baghdadis. The historical record suggests that the first of Baghdad's cafés came about in 1590, during the Abbasid reign. It was located near the Mustansiriya madrasa. Hassan Pasha's Café, founded in 1604, is also one of the most famous. In these cafés, coffee was served while people listened to the popular musical ensembles of the day.

Thomas Herbert, an Englishman who visited Baghdad in the 16th century, was surprised to discover a place called the House of Qahwa (coffee in Arabic) where "a multitude of Muslims gather to drink a thick, hot, bitter black liquor made of certain burnt seeds..."

Under the Ottoman Empire, Sultan Murad IV's interdiction of coffee was respected in Istanbul, but not in Baghdad. During the 19th century, the city had 184 cafés! There were favorite cafés for artisans, merchants, and the intelligentsia. Games such as backgammon and chess, and the ubiquitous *maqam*, were some of the entertainments offered.

During the British Mandate, the cafés became centers of revolutionary agitation. Poets recited nationalist verse and writers and activists gave public readings of the popular clandestine press.

Al-Safafir Souk

Mutanabi Street

Named after the great Arab poet, al-Mutanabi (915–965). Running perpendicular to the Tigris, Mutanabi Street gives out onto Rashid Street. On Friday mornings, the sidewalks become a used-book souk. Most are in Arabic, but there are often rare English and French books as well.

Tahrir Place (Freedom Square)

Here, a monumental fresco by the sculptor Jawad Salim dominates the scene. The over-150-foot-wide mural gives a chronological representation of various episodes of Iraqi history, up to the overthrow of the monarchy in 1958. Note: like Arabic, it reads from right to left.

Tahrir Place Souk

Here, you can find almost anything, from designer fountain pens at an unbeatable price to antique pocket watches. Opposite the mural on the edge of the square, down near the central traffic circle, there are several stores that sell antique cameras. On Fridays, the market overflows along Jumhuriya Avenue, all the way to the animal market.

Al-Safafir Souk

Still where it was in the 11th century, the artisans and merchants of the copperware market offer all kinds of decorative objects and kitchenware.

Al-Chorja Souk

This souk, the spice market, dates from the 19th century, and is located between Rashid Street and al-Khulafa Street. The best time to go there is late morning, when the market is at its most bustling. One can find rare spices and medicinal plants.

Souk of the Serai

This, the antique market, is a veritable collectors' paradise, with all manner of antiques and even old postcards.

The "Bird Market"

On Jumhuriya Avenue, this souk is a regular meeting place for animal lovers of all kinds; indeed, in this market one can buy not just birds (including live poultry, eagles, and falcons) but also dogs, cats, goldfish, and even snakes. This market literally bursts with life!

Abu Nawas Street

The poet Abu Nawas praised the virtues of wine and worldly pleasures during the reign of Harun al-Rashid. The street that bears his name runs along the Tigris from the Jumhuriya Bridge. Clients of the big hotels (the Palestine, the Sheraton, and the Baghdad) often head toward the numerous restaurants with a river view, where one can sample various versions of *masgouf*, the traditional Iraqi dish.

Masgouf is a particular way of cooking fish. In Baghdad, people prefer the Tigris carp, called the *shabbut*. Cut open along the back and skewered, it is cooked over a tamarisk wood fire, then served with a tomato and onion garnish and pita bread.

Saadun Street

Saadun Street is modern Baghdad's *Champs-Elysées*, with many shops, movie theaters, art galleries, hotels, and restaurants. Prime Minister Mohsen Saadun committed suicide on November 13, 1929, out of despair over the continued British presence in Iraq.

The Baghdad Clock

In the vast hall beneath this clock, a giant kalashnikov-shaped seesaw keeps the seconds. The many gifts that Saddam Hussein has received occupy several adjacent rooms, grouped by theme: paintings, musical instruments, and weaponry, among which is an antique sword offered by French President Jacques Chirac.

Arbataash Tamuz (14th of July) Bridge

This bridge (not to be confused with the July 17th Bridge, marking the triumph of the Ba'athist revolution) commemorates the 1958 fall of the monarchy. The bridge was destroyed during the Gulf War, and later rebuilt, in spite of the embargo. The special cables that hold the bridge were apparently imported with great difficulty.

Zawra Gardens

This vast wooded area boasts a zoo, playgrounds for children of all ages, an open-air theater, and an Olympic-sized pool. The top of a 200-foot-high tower in the gardens boasts a magnificent view of Baghdad.

Monument of Martyrs

This majestic structure commemorating civilian dead during the Iran–Iraq War consists of a pointed mosque-like dome about 150 feet high, cut in half and situated on a huge marble esplanade surrounded by water. Designed by Fattal al-Turk, a Basra-born architect, the shape suggests a split shell or a flame. It is finished in a special blue tile unique to Babylon, reminiscent of those on Babylon's Ishtar Gate.

Monument to the War Dead

The arch that covered the Tomb of the Unknown Soldier, built in 1959 on one of Saadun Street's many traffic circles, next to the 14th of Ramadan Mosque, was razed. The anonymous remains were transferred to a final resting place under a 500-ton shield that covers the impressive Monument to the War Dead built in 1982. It is located near the Zawra Gardens, next to the Hotel Rashid.

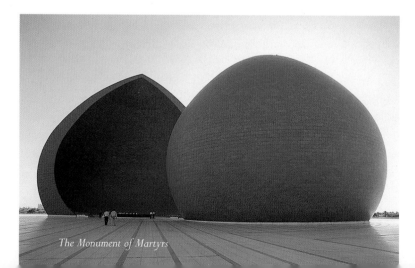

The Monument of Martyrs

——— FIVE ———

The Last Disciples of
St. John the Baptist

N ot far from the Tigris, hidden behind a barrier of reeds, at first glance nothing distinguishes one concrete building from the other villas of the well-to-do neighborhood of Qadisiyya. But at the top of the temple gate, there is a strange cross, made of two olive branches, covered with a cloth. This is Baghdad's Mandean temple (*mandi*). The Mandeans are the last disciples of St. John the Baptist.

The adobe Mandean temples photographed at the beginning of the last century have disappeared forever, but Mandean traditions are more robust. On temple days, the Mandeans put away their Western attire for the *rasta* of their ancestors: a white cotton robe, tied at the waist with a burlap cord. Their priests dress the same as in Biblical times, and deliver their sermons in a dialect derived from Aramaic.

For Mandeans, as for Christians, Sunday is a holy day. On that day, celebrants are up early, preparing the festivities in the temple courtyard. Families wait on a bench with a baby to be baptized, or accompany a bride and groom to the altar. At first glance, the cars outside in the parking lot reflect the Mandeans' reputation for affluence. But upon closer inspection, one sees that the Mandeans' luxury cars are not the newest models: since the embargo, the jewelry trade, in which Mandeans have excelled for centuries, has declined. Today, their cafés on River Street are practically all closed.

The destruction of water treatment plants during the Gulf War has also caused great distress to the Mandeans, for whom running river water is a spiritual necessity. Indeed, water from the Tigris is piped into a special pool in the temple for baptisms. The river is now heavily polluted, but the Mandeans drink it regularly; miraculously, there are few cases of illness.

The Mandeans' Mysterious Origins

The Mandeans, also called Sabeans, are a little-known sect, even though their prophet, Yahia, played an important role in the early history of Christianity. Yahia, or Yuhana, is, of course, none other than John the Baptist, who baptized Jesus in the River Jordan.

There are about 150,000 Mandeans today, 15,000 of whom live in Iraq. Information about them abound, but is not very reliable.

In the 18th century, Europeans called them the "Christians of St. John," which is curious, for Jesus is not exactly the most revered figure for the Mandeans. Indeed, they accuse Christ of having modified the original rite of baptism as practiced by Saint John, and using his ideas to create a new religion. Needless to say, relations with the Christian churches of the East have not always been good.

Since the Mandeans are a pacific people, not given to proselytizing, they eventually ceased to be considered a threat. In 1990, Pope John-Paul II granted an audience to the Mandeans' spiritual leader, Shaykh Najem; the Mandeans are now on quite cordial terms with the Vatican. But it is good to remember that the cross over the temple gate in no way refers to the Christ, but instead, to the olive branches that John the Baptist used to bless his disciples with water from the Jordan River. Arranged in a cross, with a length of cloth rolled over them, they are a sign to the faithful of the place where St. John baptized his disciples.

The ethnic origin of the Mandeans remains mysterious. Some researchers have claimed that they descend from the Kingdom of Saba, but this hypothesis has been abandoned. "Sabean" is a deformation of the word *soub'hi* referring to "those who immerse themselves" or "those who bow." In this case, the name refers to the ancient Sabeans of Harran, who bowed to the planets. The name "Mandean" comes from the Aramaic word for knowledge.

The Mother of all Religions?

The roots of Mandeism lie deep in the history of Mesopotamia: according to its adepts, it is the "mother of all religions." Scientific evidence to prove this has yet to be found, but it is true that Mandean writings show the survival of ancient Babylonian, Zoroastrian, and Manichean beliefs. The Mandean scriptures are so obscure that only initiates can understand them, and there are often quarrels as to the true meaning of sayings that have been deformed through time by countless interpretations. Some Mandeans end up abandoning their faith for this reason, and for this reason too, the High Council of Mandean spiritual leaders is trying to make the sacred texts accessible to all. A great Mandean poet, Abdul Razzaq al-Wahib, has been given the task of translating the Mandean scripture, the *Ginza Rabba*, or Great Treasure, into Arabic. It is a controversial undertaking: many Mandeans are viscerally attached to their traditions, and think that the Great Treasure should only be read in the language of their ancestors.

The Mandeans are dualists. According to their worldview and their version of genesis, at the beginning the world was divided in two: an upper world representing Life and Light, and a lower world lost in darkness. God, whom Mandeans call Manda Haiye ("Knower of Life"), decided one day to create the earth and humankind. Abathur and his son, Ptahil, two demigods, were charged with this task. They captured and chained up Ur, master of the netherworld, and the Earth then emerged from the black waters of Chaos. The different versions of the Creation share many fundamental givens; the Mandean black waters recall the "waters of death" of the Mesopotamian epic of Gilgamesh, which inspired writers of the Biblical Genesis.

Then, the demigods created Adam. But his body remained inert. To animate him, they had to go back up to the world of light to steal some sparks from the "Treasure of Life." Souls, say the Mandeans, feel imprisoned in the bodies they inhabit. Fortunately, these are but "perishable envelopes." Souls wish only to return to the true Abode of Life.

Abraham, Mandean Prophet

The Mandeans claim Abraham as their first "great baptizer." We know, according to Genesis, that the patriarch left Ur 4,000 years ago for Harran, an ancient city whose remains are located near Altinbasak, close to Urfa in southern Turkey. He then went to Palestine. The Sabeans of Harran may have been members of the tribe of Abraham who decided to remain there, and who developed beliefs centered on the stars and planets. In 830, with the arrival of Caliph al-Ma'mun, Harun's son, the Sabeans abandoned paganism. The Caliph really left them no choice: they had to convert to Islam, recanting all their beliefs, or to another religion mentioned in the Qur'an—or die. The sect then integrated the "official" Sabean sect, represented by a community living in southern Iraq, who worshipped the Book of Noah. The Sabeans' contemporary practice of praying in the direction of the Northern Star is certainly a remnant of an ancient Mesopotamian tradition.

The Sabeans who had followed Abraham to Canaan settled near the River Jordan, the source of their holy water. In their religious writings, the Jordan has a double in the Upper World of Life, like the two Iraqi rivers in the Bible. The Sabeans allegedly left the region after the "betrayal of Christ" and the execution of John the Baptist. They thus returned to their point of departure: the banks of the Euphrates River.

Mesopotamian clay tablets are mute on the subject of the Sabeans, which leads many researchers to affirm that the religion is a recent one, at least in its present configuration. The figure of Saint John might have been appropriated recently, to encourage the authorities' tolerance toward the sect. At any rate, Amara, a city located in the southern swamp region, serves as a holy city. John the Baptist may have lived there before going to Damascus; this is but conjecture.

John the Baptist

According to Flavius Josephus (67–100), Jewish historian and Roman citizen, John the Baptist was an "honest man." The Roman occupants had only one quarrel with him: his fiery sermons. Herod Antipas (20 BCE–30 CE), the Tetrarch (governor) named by Augustus, feared that John the Baptist was inciting the people to rebellion. When John had

Baptism during a Mandean wedding

the temerity to criticize the Herod's marriage to his own half-niece, Herodiad, Herod had John the Baptist arrested, but this was not enough for his new wife. She took advantage of a promise made to her daughter Salome to demand his head. So it was that John the Baptist was decapitated in the year 27 or 28 in the fortress of Macheronte, east of the Jordan. According to the historian Abu Jafar al-Tabari (839-923), John's head started speaking on the platter and his blood boiled for centuries. In olden times, Palestinians crossing the gate of the Column (or Damascus Gate, the northern entrance to Jerusalem) would toss some stones as a gesture to calm the spirit of the prophet and martyr.

After the death of Saint John the Baptist, Jesus took refuge in Galilee. When he first heard about Christ's activities, Antipas thought Saint John had come back to life (Luke 9, 7–9).

John's head is buried in Damascus, in what was later to become the principal mosque of the Omayyads. His body is said to have been interred at Sebaste, in Samaria; digs are currently being conducted in Jordan to determine the true site of his tomb. For Mandeans, the tomb of their prophet is not very important, for he was not interred according to tradition. More important is that his soul resides in the "Country of Light." There are even doubts among the Mandeans as to the true circumstances of John's death. According to legend, another prisoner replaced Yahia at the last minute. Interestingly, a substitution hypothesis has also been voiced about Jesus himself.

The New Testament is rather veiled about the subject of John the Baptist's religion. There is a lack of agreement, too, about the true relations between John and his cousin, Jesus. The apostles could have said more, and one wonders why they did not. After all, most of them were formerly members of John's entourage, before joining Jesus Christ's. We might know more once all the Dead Sea Scrolls are made public.

Death, Liberation for the Soul

The worst thing for a Mandean is to have to leave this world without a last baptism and without the *rasta*. In this respect, the Mandean faith is undoubtedly the only one in which last rites are administered before death. Actually, older devotees, or those who fear accidental death for example, can receive them from a priest; the only condition being total sexual abstinence from that moment on.

The waters of the sacrament free the souls of the dying. In the afterlife, a Mandean changes his first name. He or she takes a secret patronym, established at birth. The soul has to pass seven tests before entering the *Alme Denhoro* (the Mandean heaven), and taking its place in the "Treasure of Life."

Christ's resurrection, which permeates the New Testament, is absent from the Mandean faith. Returning to the body would mean being limited once again. Impure souls must cross a sort of purgatory, and arrive in Paradise only after being completely washed of their sins.

The Circumcision of Abraham

River water is omnipresent in the Mandean faith. "Life put life in the water," according to their saying, and placed its essential virtues in the baptismal River. This is why baptism is repeated at every important occasion, in order to purify the body and soul, and protect them from Evil.

Mandeans are not supposed to modify their appearance, which they consider sacred, as it is God-given. They are thus forbidden from circumcision, and even from having their tonsils removed. To explain Abraham's circumcision, the Mandeans say that the operation was performed for medical reasons; having automatically lost his right to baptize people, he then left Ur forever. In ancient times, circumcision was sometimes interpreted as a mark of infamy, imposed as a sign of submission to an enemy god. It is also possible that the Patriarch, who was vehemently opposed to idolatry and to King Nimrud, might have been forced into circumcision. (Nimrud, a descendant of Noah, had returned to paganism. He was supposed to possess the tunics of Adam and Eve, which were made of the skin of the mythical leviathan and gave their wearer supernatural powers.)

Strict Rules

Most of the Mandeans who lived in southern Iraq have ended up in Baghdad. The drastic conditions created by the embargo have led them to rely even more upon themselves and each other. Celibacy is frowned upon; indeed, polygamy is encouraged, without limit. As for divorce, it is forbidden, but priests can authorize a form of separation. Intermarriage has created a strong community bond, like that within a clan or tribe.

The Mandeans are led by a Shaykh, but the supreme rank of *Rabbani* has never been conferred, the Mandeans having judged that no one since Yahia has been worthy of it. A mere mortal could never, in their view, attain the required state of grace.

Food taboos are stricter for the Mandeans than for either Jews or Muslims. Like them, the Mandeans do not eat pork. In fact, they do not eat any furred animals, and their respect for life forbids them from eating female animals. They can only eat mutton and chicken, and only after having thoroughly washed the animal before cutting its throat. Needless to say, a Mandean casts a wary eye on any meal not prepared within the community. They can drink alcohol in moderation.

Priesthood is handed down from father to son. The obligations of Mandean clerics are even stricter than for lay people. The future priest must pass strict scrutiny; any physical imperfection is forbidden. Mandean priests lead ascetic lives: they only eat what they have prepared, and drink only water from the Tigris. Alcohol, tea, and coffee are forbidden. They can only take medicine through the skin, and never cut their hair.

The Mandean calendar begins in April, the month of the creation and of the birth of Yahia. The year is otherwise divided into twelve months of four weeks. The main religious holiday is Panja, in April. It lasts five days. Families stay at home, preparing symbolic repasts for the dead.

Mandean Marriage

We return to the courtyard of Shaykh Kadur's *mandi*, where the high priest of the Mandeans of Baghdad officiates every Sunday, surrounded

Mandean wedding on the banks of the Tigris

by his assistants. In the courtyard, husbands and brides waiting their turn adjust their *rastas* for the ceremony. Mandeans are not allowed to marry outside their religion: those who disobey this rule are rejected by the community. After daubing the young people's foreheads with water and sesame oil, the Shaykh puts a sprig of myrrh in their hair, as a symbol of the soul's immortality.

The shaykh and the groom enter a reed framework in the *mandi*'s courtyard, which represents the couple's future household. He offers the groom a bowl of *pichta* and a bowl of *mambugha*, the holy bread and water. Prayers are pronounced celebrating the "Treasure of Life." The priest then solemnly shakes the groom's hand, puts his own hand on his head, and intones a series of praises to Manda of Haiye. Someone in the audience shatters an earthen pot in order to scare away evil spirits.

During this time, the bride waits in a nearby room. Women of the community have tested her virginity, and her husband-to-be is soon with her, as well as the two families. The couple is seated back to back. Another earthen pot is broken at the entrance, the priest takes the heads of the couple and lightly brings them together. His prayer is drowned out by the shouts of the parents. They seem to be mocking their children, but actually they are encouraging them, shouting things like "the one who hits hardest will control the household!" The ceremony ends in the waters of the Tigris, where all the participants take a ritual dip.

Aside from their religious life, the Mandeans are totally integrated in Iraqi society, as jewelers, but also as professors, artists, or army officers. Sabean learned men have gone down in history. One of them, Thabit Ibn Qara al-Harrani, who lived at the court of al-Ma'mun, had a considerable influence on medicine, astronomy, and religious thought. Under the Abbasid reign, Mandean scientists were well known. While they didn't find the philosophical stone or the elixir of youth, a collective quest of the Middle Ages, Mandean alchemists were led to important discoveries in metal alloys.

In the year 2000, Baghdadi Mandeans celebrated the new

millenium. But for them, they have been separated, not from the Christ, but from their own prophet, Yahia—John the Baptist—for all these years.

The Mandean Holy Writings

The principal sacred texts of the Mandeans are the *Ginza Rabba*, the Book of John, and the Mandean liturgy.

The *Ginza Rabba* or "Great Treasure" contains the books of Adam, Seth, and Sem, and prayers to the Creator. It is divided into two parts, the "Left" *Ginza* and the "Right" *Ginza*. The first is a theology of life. The second is devoted to the fate of the soul and the description of its return to the "Treasure of Life"—a theology of death.

The Book of John gathers teachings of the prophet. It is a compilation of sermons.

The Mandean liturgy is an ensemble of chants and hymns for baptism and the rising of the soul to the World of Light.

The oldest surviving copy of the *Ginza*, carefully handed down over the generations, has unfortunately been stolen.

The cave where Abraham was born, in Borsippa

SIX

Near Baghdad

Ctesiphon (Taq-e-Qisra)

Located about 19 miles (30km) south of Baghdad, Ctesiphon was founded opposite Seleucia in 144 BCE by the Parthian king, Mithridatus I (170–138 BCE), who had made it his winter capital.

Arab geographers called the region al-Mada'in, meaning simply the "place of cities." Indeed, in addition to Ctesiphon and Seleucia, there were five other cities in the region. On either side of the Tigris, the vestiges of some of these cities have been unearthed: Rumiyya, where Caliph al-Mansur once stayed, as well as Sabat, Baharasur, and Tell Baruda.

Ctesiphon was attacked several times by the Romans and occupied by the Emperor Trajan. But the Romans were never able to maintain a foothold in Mesopotamia. Ctesiphon was taken by Ardashir (226–241), founder of the Persian Sassanid dynasty. His son, Shapur I (241–272) moved there himself. It is thought that the White Palace, of which one wing, called Taq-e-Qisra (throne of Chosroes, or Koshrow in Persian) survives, was built during the reign of Shapur I.

Its architecture is reminiscent of the temples of Hatra, a city in the north of Iraq that Shapur I had taken and destroyed. Shapur I had even given orders to slaughter the entire population of Hatra, saving only the artisans he would need to embellish Ctesiphon.

The palace and its gigantic *iwan* were restored by Chosroes I (531–579). In winter, a 1,000-square-yard rug covered the floor. "Chosroes' Rug" was made of silk, gold, and silver thread, and decorated with precious stones.

According to legend, one of the towers of the White Palace collapsed on the day of the Prophet Mohammed's birth. This event was

The arch of Ctesiphon

interpreted as a warning from Allah to the powerful Sassanid King Chosroes II (590–628).

Chosroes II is known for having torn up a letter from Mohammad inviting him to convert to Islam. And Christians have their own complaints, too: they accused him of having used wood from Christ's cross, stolen from Jerusalem, for his throne.

To the left of the *iwan*, the façade of the palace is still standing. In 1909, the right wing collapsed during a flood of the Tigris. The arch is 40 yards high. The elliptical vault, 50 yards deep, is the largest and oldest known in the world.

In May 1908, the Oriental scholar Louis Massignon recovered his faith before the Palace of Ctesiphon. Accused of spying by British archeologists who wanted an excuse to get rid of a competitor, he had been arrested by the Turks, and his life threatened on the way back from the Castle of al-Uqaidir. Thrown into a boat going up the Tigris without further ceremony, he had attempted to commit suicide. It was then that he had a revelation. Later, in *The Idea of God*, he wrote:

> The anonymous Arab who visited me, one evening in May, in front of the Taq, on the Tigris, who came into my prison cell, where I was tightly bound, after two escape attempts, caught the fire in my heart that the knife had missed. He cauterized my despair, smelted it into hope, like the phosphorescence of a fish surfacing from the deep....

Ctesiphon was ravaged in 628 by the Byzantines. Chosroes fled, only to be assassinated by his son, Khawad II. The taking of the city by Muslims in 637, after the victory of al-Qadisiyya, signaled the end of Persian domination over Iraq. As for the famous arch, worrisome cracks have appeared since the 1991 Gulf War, from the sonic boom of American fighter jets, but even after the 2003 war, it was still standing.

The Tomb of Salman al-Farisi

Nearby, at Salman Pak (the Pure, in Farsi), about a mile from Taq-e-Qisra, one can find the tomb of Salman al-Farisi (the Persian), one of the closest companions of the Prophet, and the first Persian to convert to Islam.

Salman (whose real name is Rozeba) was from Jiyye, a city near Ispahan. Born into a Zoroastrian family, he converted early to Christianity in Syria. But when the bishop of Mosul announced the apparition of a prophet in Arabia, Salman went to meet him. Taken prisoner along the way, he was sold as a slave to a Jew in Yathrib (later Medina). One day, Salman learned that the Prophet would be attending a funeral, and vowed to meet him there. Once at the funeral, Salman looked for the Prophet's distinguishing mark, called "the Sign of the Prophet," which Mohammad had on his back. Perhaps guessing his thoughts, Mohammad uncovered his shoulder, allowing the Persian to see who he was. Salman immediately kissed the sacred mark, then told the Prophet his story. He converted to Islam, and Mohammad gave him the name Salman, declaring him "neither a Persian, nor an Arab, but one of us (Ahl al-Bayt: one of the family)."

The Prophet helped Salman buy back his freedom. His price had been set by his angry master at 40 ounces of gold and three hundred date palms. Mohammad asked his companions to find the requisite number of palm saplings, and helped Salman to plant them. Then, he placed in his mouth a gold ingot that had been found in a nearby mine. The price of Salman's freedom had been met. Not long after Salman was freed, he was instrumental in saving the city of Medina from an attack by the Koraish tribe in 627. Salman had the idea of protecting the oasis from enemy cavalry by digging a huge moat. The ensuing battle is called the Day of the Moat in Islamic history. While digging the moat, the laborers found a rock that was impossible to extract. Mohammad came to their aid, cracking the huge rock into pieces on the third blow of his axe. At each blow, a stroke of lightning flew out in a different direction. The first two showed Mohammad the castles of Yemen and Syria. He interpreted this as a sign from Allah to go and conquer these lands. The third illuminated Chosroes' palace at Ctesiphon: the gates of the Orient were opening to Mohammed. Salman died in Iraq during the reign of Caliph Uthman, at the governor's post of al-Madain (Ctesiphon). When he felt the end drawing near, he had his house perfumed with musk. Then he told his wife he was expecting important visitors, and sent her away. For some Muslims, the visitors were envoys from Paradise sent to accompany Salman, for Mohammad had promised him a place there. His wife found him dead upon her return.

Only Muslims can enter Salman's mausoleum. In another room of the sanctuary, two of the Prophet's companions, whose graves were threatened by flooding from the Tigris, are also interred.

The mosque was slightly damaged during the 1991 war. It has been repaired and further restoration is also underway.

The Panorama of al-Qadisiyya

This 90-foot-tall structure, closely resembling a defensive tower, has a commanding view. The decisive battles in the Muslims' conquest of Persia are visually represented by a series of bas-reliefs. This building had been completely looted by May of 2003, when a team went to inspect the damage from the war to important archeological sites.

Aqarquf (Dur Kurigalzu)

This city, 20 miles (32 km) from Baghdad, was built by the Kassite king Kurigalzu I, in about 1400 BCE. He gave his name to the capital, a first in the history of Mesopotamia. This king was a contemporary of the Egyptian Pharaoh Amenophis II, who financed the city's construction in large part.

Egypt also helped the Kassites deal with the powerful Mittanian (which at the time extended from the Zagros mountains to Palestine) and Assyrian kingdoms. Indeed, diplomatic and commercial relations between the two countries developed steadily until the reign of Amenophis IV (Ikhnaton, 1364–1347 BCE).

What is left of the ziggurat stands over 180 feet tall, and can be seen from afar, and notably from the Amman/Baghdad highway, which crosses the Abu Gharib region. Many travellers down through the ages have mistaken it for the fabled tower of Babel.

The base of the ziggurat, with its monumental staircase, has been restored. The edifice has resisted time and humidity thanks to a rather ingenious construction device: reeds disposed between layers throughout the structure helped ventilate the unbaked clay bricks. Iraqi archeologists have excavated the base of the tower, uncovering remains of the royal palace and several temples, where they found a sizeable statue of Kurigalzu.

Tell Harmal (Shaduppum)

In the second millenium BCE, Shaduppum was part of the kingdom of Eshnuna. This city's origins go back to the fourth millenium BCE. Situated in the Diyala River valley, it is five miles (8 km) northeast of Baghdad (Tell Asmar).

At Tell Harmal, Iraqis have discovered a Code of Laws written in Akkadian, dating from the reign of Dadusha, King of Eshnuna in the 17th century BCE – in other words, a code of law that significantly predates that of Hammurabi. Four baked clay statues of lions that guarded the gates of the temples of Hani and Nisiba have been unearthed, as well as the *cella*, the section of the sanctuary where the gods were represented, and clay tablets. On one of them, a graph was drawn of a theorem later attributed to Euclid, the Greek mathematician who lived in Alexandria 1,500 years later.

SEVEN

From Baghdad to Najaf

Babylon, the "Pearl of Kingdoms"

The ruins of the Babylon of Hammurabi (1792–1750 BCE), a contemporary of Abraham, are hidden 55 miles (90 km) south of Baghdad, near Hilla—40 yards underground. The visible remains are those of the city built by Nabopolassar (625–605 BCE), "King of the Country of the Sea," and by the great Nabuchadnezzar II (652–605 BCE).

Thirty years ago, Babylon was a sorry sight. Archaeologists and thieves had taken almost everything and ruined the site. Local residents had used ancient bricks to build their houses. The famous lion, eroded by the desert winds and damaged by German diggers frustrated by their failure to bring it back to Berlin, slouched among a pile of ruins.

Today, Babylon has been reborn from its ashes. The summer palace, the temples of Ishtar and of Nabushcari, the ramparts, a Greek amphitheater, and the "House of Marvels of the People" have all undergone partial restoration. The results are quite spectacular, especially if one imagines the effort it must have taken to rebuild such an ensemble in the aftermath of the war with Iran. Saddam Hussein, determined to hark back to Iraq's past glory, spared no cost. The bricks come from local factories that have respected the ancient brick-making procedures. If you use your imagination, you can almost hear the prophecies of Daniel, and the echo of the chants of people climbing the great staircase of Etemenaki, the "House of the Foundation of Heaven and Earth," the ziggurat better known by its biblical name, the Tower of Babel.

The First Great Centralized Empire

Babylon (from *bab ilou*, the gate of God) was founded in the 24th century BCE by King Sumu-Abom of the Amorites, a Semitic people. The city was to owe its development and its influence to its strategic position between the two poles of civilization in Mesopotamia, and along the Euphrates, already a long-navigated river. Babylon would enter history after the fall of Ur in 2003 BCE, under Hammurabi.

Hammurabi (1728–1685 BCE), a brilliant diplomat, extended Babylon's imperial influence to include a territory roughly equivalent to present-day Iraq. He is most known for his code of laws, written on numerous stelae, the first of which was discovered in 1902 in Susa (Iran) by French archaeologists. It is now on display in the Louvre.

After Hammurabi's death, Babylon was overrun by a series of invading peoples: Assyrians from the north, Kassites and Elamites from the east, and the swamp peoples from the south. All would end up succumbing to the attractions of Babylonian civilization. The last Amorite king was overthrown by Hittites from Anatolia, who would destroy Baghdad in 1594 BCE, taking with them the statue of Marduk, the supreme god of the Babylonians. He is represented by a dragon with the head of a snake.

Years of Fire and Blood

A period of anarchy and decline now plagued Babylon, until the Kassite king, Agum Kakrimeh, took the city and brought back the stolen statue of Marduk. These mountain people from the Zagros Mountains of Persia reigned a half a millenium, until the arrival of the Elamites. This time, the statue of Marduk was "imprisoned" in Susa. Nabuchadnezzar I would be the one to retrieve it this time.

In 1234 BCE, Assyrians destroyed the city, and Tiglat Pileser III (known in the Old Testament as Pul) had himself proclaimed king of the new Assyrian Empire in 731 BCE.

In 689 BCE, after the accession to power of Marduk Apal Idin II (Merodach Baladan in the Bible), the ruthless Assyrian king, Sennacherib (704–6781 BCE), son of Sargon II, destroyed the city again. Babylon would be reborn under his son, Assharaddon, whose mother was a former priestess of Babylon (680 BCE).

In 625 BCE, King Nabopolassar founded a new dynasty. Allied with the Medes, he crushed the Assyrians. Then, under Nabuchadnezzar II (in the 6th century BCE), Babylon finally achieved its golden age. In fact, the prophet Jeremy described the city as "a golden cup in the hands of the Lord to make the whole world drunk."

His son Nabonid fell under a Persian plot. Cyrus took the city without difficulty in 539 BCE with the help of the priests of Marduk and the Babylonian Jews, whom he had promised a safe return to Jerusalem.

The Persians would be a benevolent presence, but not for long. Following a popular revolt, Xerxes (485–464 BCE) destroyed the city and notably the ziggurat.

The Dream of Alexander

After having defeated Darius at Erbil in 331 BCE, Alexander the Great set up camp near Babylon. Impressed by the field of ruins, he recruited 10,000 workers to excavate the ruins of the Tower of Babel and decided to build the capital of his new empire there. But he died of malaria upon his return from the Indus Valley in June 323 BCE, without having achieved his goal.

Seleucos Nicator I, his successor, preferred to build a new city about 45 miles (72 km) from Babylon, on the right bank of the Tigris. He called the city Seleucia.

Samiramis and the Legend of Babylon

Throughout antiquity, there were numerous legends about Samiramis, the mythical founding queen of Babylon. According to one of the better known, she was the daughter of a mermaid goddess, Derceta, and of a young man who worshipped her. Her mother, ashamed at her union with a mere mortal, supposedly killed the father on the day of her delivery, and abandoned the baby in an inhospitable desert.

The newborn baby survived, however, and was brought up by doves, until the day when Simma, royal shepherd-in-chief, found her and adopted her. One day, Onnes, governor of Syria, was inspecting the royal stables: when he saw her, he immediately fell in love.

Samiramis accompanied her husband to the court of Ninus, the king of Nineveh. Soon, Onnes, who had set out on a military expedition to Bactria (in what is today northern Afghanistan), asked Samiramis to join him, for the campaign was proving to be a long one, and he was lonely without his wife. The city of Bactres (today Balkh), with its strong walls, was not giving up easily.

Upon arrival in the military camp, Samiramis became involved in the fighting. She organized a commando that succeeded in taking the fortress-city by surprise. Impressed, King Ninus promptly awarded her with jewels—and his love. When Onnes refused the king's request that he divorce Samiramis so that she could be his, the king threatened to have his eyes gouged out. Instead, Onnes committed suicide.

Ninus was then free to marry Samiramis, who soon gave birth to Ninyas, a boy. Not much time passed before the king was poisoned—speculation had it, by his wife.

Samiramis now reigned supreme. But she never married, doubtless afraid of losing her throne. It is said that she chose her consorts from among the handsomest of the soldiers, and she put them to death when they no longer pleased her.

To commemorate the munificence of her reign, Samiramis decided to build a new city. This would be Babylon, a gigantic city spanning both sides of the Euphrates, with city walls so thick that several chariots could run side by side along the ramparts. Two palaces faced each other on either side of the river; they were linked by an underground tunnel, which had entailed diverting the Euphrates. Legend says that Babylon was built in 365 days, by two million workers.

Once this magnificent feat had been achieved, Samiramis set out to conquer India, but this time her army fared less well. Learning that her son was getting ready to oust her from power, she sped back to Nineveh. Once there, the queen ceded the throne to her son, and locked herself in her apartments.

She is said to have opened the window and flown out, changed into a dove, to join a flock that had been awaiting her on the roof. Samiramis, the legendary queen, is said to have reigned 42 years.

Some historians say that Samiramis did indeed exist, but that the historical Sumuramat, an Assyrian queen, reigned only five years over the Assyrian empire, in the 7th century BCE.

The Gate of Ishtar

Ishtar, the goddess of fertility and war, is the wife of Ashur, the national god of the Assyrians. The gate pictured is unfortunately a reproduction; the original is on display at the Pergamon Museum in Berlin. German archaeologists took twenty years to reconstruct the upper level. The lacquered bricks had been crushed into thousands of pieces. Some of them remained in Istanbul, and ended up being used as foundation material for the Turkish city.

The Gate of Ishtar

The Temple of Nin-Makh

Near Ishtar's Gate, the temple of Nin-Makh (the Great Lady) has been restored. One can see many vestiges of the ancient walls, which were made of dried bricks.

The Procession Road

The yearly parade, held on the eighth day of the New Year, was called Ai-ibur-shabu, in other words "That the enemy may not cross." The king, holding the hand of the statue of Marduk, walked to the temple of the New Year (Bit Akitu), located outside the city limits. Three days later, after having spent the last night on top of the ziggurat with a young woman chosen by the priests, Marduk recovered his usual place in the E-sag-il, or temple of Marduk.

The Procession Road is best seen starting from Ishtar's Gate, going toward the temple of Marduk. Long ago, the road, whose walls have been restored with their decorations of horned dragons and bulls, occupied three levels. It crossed the Euphrates, which at the time passed through the city. The reconstruction of the wooden bridge is on the drawing board.

Babylon Destroyed and Restored

The commemorative plaque on the palace at Babylon provides an interesting encapsulation of the forces of history and myth at play in this ancient spot.

The text begins with a quote from the Book of Isaiah: "Babylon, the pearl of kingdoms, the jewel, the pride of the Chaldeans, will, like Sodom and Gomorrah, be cursed by God. It will never again be peopled, down through the generations... I will sweep it away with the wind of destruction..." In 689 BCE, Sennacherib continued in this apocalyptic vein: "I was like the wind heralding the tempest... I was destroying the city utterly, leaving no house, not even a foundation, standing... I burned everything...I flattened it better than any flood ever could, so that no one would ever remember this city and its temples."

In 1989, after the long war against Iran, Saddam Hussein added his own piece: "I rebuilt Babylon, I raised the walls of Nabuchadnezzar and the temples of Ishtar, Nabu, and Nin-Makh in the years 1988–89, to give back to the Iraqi people its past glory."

The Museum

Most of the vestiges of Babylon discovered since the end of the 19th century are in western museums. Only the objects that have been found recently by Iraqi archaeologists are on display.

A huge model of Babylon, however, gives a good idea of the size and wealth of the ancient city. A series of paintings represents the famous Hanging Gardens of Babylon, a ritual procession, and the Tower of Babel as it has been diversely imagined down through the centuries.

Though the museum, the director's house, the gift shop, and library were all looted and partly burned in the aftermath of the 2003 war, the damage was apparently confined by a guard who held off looters with a sickle.

The Lion of Babylon

This enigmatic statue represents a lion standing over a man on the ground. The man is pushing away the jaws of the beast with one hand, and a huge paw with the other. The Lion of Babylon was either a Hittite statue from the middle of the second millenium BCE or brought back from southern Syria. It now stands near the place where it was unearthed.

The Tower of Babel

Nothing is left of the legendary ziggurat, except a square trench surrounding the foundations—a bit disappointing! Fortunately, we know what it looked like, thanks to the description of the Greek historian Herodotus (5th century

BCE), who climbed the ziggurat's fabled steps. It was about 90 yards high, with seven levels. A spiral staircase wound around the structure, with areas set up for people to rest. A temple stood at the summit. Inside, a table made of gold was supposed to be the place where the god Marduk consorted with the woman chosen by his priests.

The bricks of the tower, like those of many of Babylon's historical sites, were used to build nearby villages and cities, notably Hilla.

The Palace of Nabuchadnezzar

The palace possessed over 200 rooms and courtyards, linked by vast hallways. It housed the royal apartments, administrative buildings, the harem, and shops, whose ruins were long mistaken for those of the Hanging Gardens.

The throne room, 50 yards long and 16 yards wide, was covered with varnished bricks. Alexander the Great is said to have died here.

The Hanging Gardens

According to legend, the Hanging Gardens of Babylon, one of the Seven Wonders of the Ancient World, were built by Nabuchadnezzar to please his wife Amytis, a Mede princess who was homesick for the mountains and gardens of her native land. The park and tiered gardens were irrigated by an aqueduct.

The Summer Palace

Just 800 yards from the site of ancient Babylon, going toward Baghdad, one passes the enormous Tell Babil, where ventilation shafts have been discovered. Archaeologists presume that this was the site of a palace designed especially for habitation in extremely hot weather.

Greek Amphitheater

Built under the Seleucids (321–141 BCE) and restored for the inauguration of the Festival of Babylon in 1988, the ancient amphitheater is the venue for an annual event featuring music and theater from around the world.

Courtyard of Nabuchadnezzar's Palace

The Walls of Babylon

Going toward Baghdad, about 500 yards from the fork, one can see the vestiges of the walls of Babylon. The outer wall, 20 feet thick and ten miles (16 km) long, ringed the city.

The Tomb of Ezekiel

Ezekial, the Hebrew prophet who was exiled by Nabuchadnezzar to Tel-Aviv "on the River Kebar" is buried at Kiffle, about 15 miles (24 km) from Hilla, between Babylon and Najaf. Mentioned in the Qur'an under the name Dhu I-Kiffle, his tomb is also a holy site for Muslims. Its Buwayhid-epoch dome is visible from afar.

Ezekial (with Moses and Jesus) is the only prophet to have resuscitated a dead man. According to the tradition, he brought back to life those that had been smitten by God for refusing to fight the non-believers.

In the Old Testament, the prophet tells (in 593 BCE) that he saw

Heaven open up before his eyes, and an enormous thundercloud filled with blazing flame come out. (Some think Ezekial was the first man to have seen a UFO.)

The village of Kiffle was inhabited until 1950 by a small Jewish community. A pilgrimage took place there for the Jewish New Year (Rosh Hashanah). Its souk is the only known souk to have a vaulted wooden roof, with ventilation holes that keep the building very pleasant, even in the middle of summer.

Ezekial's mausoleum is situated at the end of a passage down the middle of the souk. It gives out onto the ruins of an Abbasid mosque, of which only the 12th-century minaret, decorated with sculpted bricks and Kufic calligraphy, is still standing. Its top is ringed by a honeycombed balustrade.

Near Ezekial's sanctuary at Kiffle

Near the gate of the mausoleum, one will find an entrance to a tunnel about which legends abound; it has been walled in. In front of the mausoleum stands an ancient synagogue, its walls covered in inscriptions from the Torah. The monument to Ezekial is in an adjoining room. Ancient paintings line the ceiling of the dome. Caliph Ali, who lived at Kufa, is said to have knelt before Ezekial's tomb.

Another room is reserved for five of Ezekial's disciples, who were imprisoned with him after the Second Exodus, in 597 BCE. The mausoleum is supposedly built on the site of the prison where they were buried.

Between these two rooms, a space has been set up for those who come here to pray, for in addition to the illustrious Hebrews, one of the Qur'an's legendary characters, al-Qidr, the "Green Imam," is said to have made an appearance here.

The Kiffle souk used to belong to a famous Iraqi Jewish family, the Sassoon Ezekials, comparable in status to the European Rothschilds. The Sassoon brothers immigrated, one to London where he was made a baron; the other to Bombay. In association with another brother, who remained in Baghdad, they were able to amass a sizeable fortune.

Sassoon Ezekial, first minister of finance of the new Iraqi government (October 27, 1920) under King Faisal I, is buried with his wife and sister under a dilapidated house near the mausoleum.

Sippar (Abu Abba)

Sippar is one of the world's oldest cities; it is mentioned both in Herodotus and the Bible. Some archaeologists think that it existed before the Flood, and that the ruins of Akkad might lie underneath its foundations.

The site, which is about 30 miles (48 km) from Baghdad, near Yussufiya, includes notably the remains of a ziggurat, as well as those of a temple to Shamas, the sun god. Its walls are made of clay brick, held together by tar. It was built so that the rays of the sun would strike it all day long.

In 1986, an Iraqi archaeological expedition discovered in one of the rooms of the temple 56 shelves containing Sumerian clay tablets, classified by subject. This library has been shown to be older than that of King Ashurbanipal. At the end of the 19th century, Hormuzd Rassam, an Iraqi archaeologist, had unearthed over 50,000 such clay tablets, and done great damage to the site, in his search for a fabled replica of Noah's Ark made of gold.

Kish (Al-Uhaimir)

The city of Kish dates from the time of al-Obeid, around 4000 BCE. It began to take on importance around 2900 BCE, attaining its apogee toward 2700–2600 BCE. One of Mesopotamia's oldest palaces has been found there. The kings of Kish were the only ones to hold the title "King of Sumer."

The first great movement of Mesopotamian unification had as its focal point Kish, which is just east of Babylon, about 25 miles (40 km) from Hilla. A high official of Semitic origin, Sargon, seized power in the 26th century BCE. "Shuruqin," the "legitimate ruler" would extend his territory to include all of Mesopotamia, Elam, the region of Susa in Persia, Dilmun (Bahrain), Syria, and Assyria. He is thought to have occupied the Mediterranean islands of Cyprus and Crete.

Sargon, nicknamed the "King of Four Regions," would abandon Kish to found Akkad (Agadeh), as well as a dynasty that would prove one of the most illustrious in Mesopotamian history. The site of Akkad has not been located to this day.

Kish is known as al-Uhaimir (the Red City), in reference to its ziggurat made of red bricks. Its sanctuaries were dedicated to the goddess Ninlil. They were rebuilt by Nabuchadnezzar II and Nabonid. Today, however, there remain only a few scattered ruins.

Etana, a mythical king of Kish (1st dynasty), was known in a legend as "the priest who ascended to Heaven."

In 1925, a Frenchman named Watelin discovered a necropolis under a clay deposit dating from a flood known to have occurred in 3000 BCE, similar to a necropolis found at Ur.

Placing the First Stone: A Mesopotamian Tradition

Placing the first stone, or groundbreaking, is a Mesopotamian tradition dating from 2600 BCE. Plugs, or plaques, of bronze, wood, clay, or stone, protected by tarred palm leaves, and bearing the names of the kings who ordered the structures to be built, as well as the dates of construction, allow for a precise dating of nearly all the temples and buildings unearthed in Iraq.

A temple's site, its design, and the start of construction were not left to chance. Priests would make the decisions based on various auspices, the chosen site would be purified by fire, and the temple foundations anointed with oil, gold, and gems. The groundbreaking ceremony was complete with prayers, animal sacrifices, and the participation of the king.

Around 2300 BCE, the Sumerians added to their commemorative plaques a statuette representing the king carrying construction materials in a basket on his head. It was planted in the ground with libations of honey and sour milk. The pointed end of the statue that the king drove into the ground, was supposed to anchor the temple for all time, and protect it from the forces of evil.

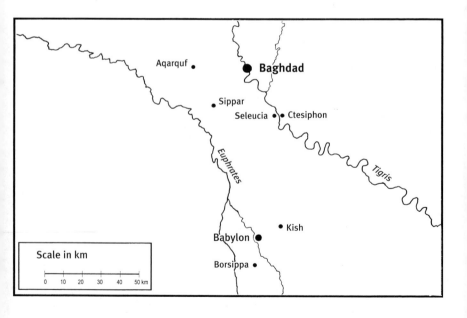

The Cave of Abraham

Situated on a branch of the Euphrates River, the ruins of a seven-story ziggurat, Eurmeiminanki (the House of the Seven Drivers of Heaven and Earth) were long mistaken for those of the Tower of Babel. The site, ten miles (16 km) southwest of Babylon, is quite difficult to reach. It is better to follow the signs for Abraham's sanctuary rather than the road for Birs Nimrud (formerly Borsippa).

The ziggurat is still 50 yards high, with one of the temple walls standing at the summit. Some say a comet smashed into the edifice, provoking a fire the bricks bear traces of today. Others say that a French archaeologist, in his hurry to find treasure, caused the damage with dynamite.

Borsippa boasted a great many sanctuaries, among which the temple of Mabu, god of scribes, discovered in 1902 by the German archaeologist Robert Koldewey. On the hill near the ziggurat, there is a sanctuary on the site of a cave where Moses is said to have been raised, hiding from the massacre of the Hebrews ordered by Nimrud.

The site of Borsippa seen from Bins Nimrud

Sargon Saved from the Waters
Mesopotamian Mythology and the Bible

"I am Sargon, the mighty king, ruler of Akkad. My mother was a priestess; I did not know my father... My city was Azupiranu, located on the banks of the Euphrates River. My mother gave birth to me secretly, and placed me in a reed basket, which she sealed with bitumen. She abandoned me to the River, but the River did not drown me. Instead, it took me to Akki, the douser. Out of the goodness of his heart, Akki adopted me and raised me as his son. Akki, the douser, taught me to be a gardener. And Ishtar fell in love with me..."

An Assyrian tablet narrating this legend was found in Egypt, in Ikhnaton's palace. Ikhnaton (Amenophet IV) was the founder of a monotheistic cult that predated the departure of Moses for Palestine.

"Sargon, king of Akkad, defied Uruk in battle. He took Lugalzaggizi prisoner, put the yoke on him, and chained him to the gate of Enlil's temple. He defied Ur and Lagash, and drove their armies to the sea. He washed his sword in the sea. He defied Uma. The citizens of Akkad mastered and governed all the land down to the Lower Sea, and Mari and Elam submitted to Sargon."

Kufa

With Basra, Kufa was one of the first cities built in Iraq by the Muslim conquerors. It was founded in 638, under Caliph Omar, by Saad Abi Waqqas, who defeated the Persians at al-Qadisiyya. The site had been chosen for its pleasant microclimate, its proximity to the Euphrates, and generally strategic position in the region.

To the west, Kufa faced the desert and Hira, a city that has disappeared today. It served the Muslims as a rear base for expeditions against Persia.

Under the Umayyads, Kufa was home to over 50 mosques. It was an important center of religious, intellectual, and commercial activity. Arabic writing was perfected there, under a style that would later be called Kufic. Its caravanserai, called the *kunasa* (depot), had an immense souk; poetry competitions were held there.

The people of Kufa quickly took Ali's side in the war of succession to the caliphate. They provided decisive support to Ali in the Battles of the Camel and of Siffin in 658, and after his victory Ali decided to make Kufa his capital.

But the Prophet's son-in-law was to be fatally wounded in the Great Mosque only three years later, purportedly stabbed with a poisoned dagger by a Karijite, to avenge the death of his parents at the hand of Ali's troops. Others have affirmed that the Karijite was under the spell of a woman who demanded Ali's death as precondition for marriage... For a long time, upon the anniversary of Ali's murder, the people of Kufa lit a ceremonial bonfire on the grave of his assassin.

After Ali's death, Kufa became the cradle of Shi'a Islam. The first Abbasid caliph took up residence in 749, after having massacred the inhabitants. His successors chose to set up their capitals elsewhere, fearing for their security in Kufa.

Kufa was ravaged three times by the Karmats in the early 10th century, until it progressively lost its importance. Today, one can visit

The sanctuary of Imam Ali Ibn Abi Taleb in Najaf

Ali's house, and the great mosque, which has been restored. According to a legend dating from the 4th Caliph, this religious edifice was built on the site where Abraham and the prophet Enoch (Idriss in the Qur'an) prayed together. Noah supposedly lived in the area as well. In the 19th century, an ancient carpenter's tool, said to belong to Noah himself, hung on the roof of the sanctuary. The site is easily visible in the courtyard of the mosque.

The great Arab philosopher, al-Kindi, a teacher and adviser to Caliph al-Ma'mun, was born in 801 at Kufa. He wrote a number of works on various subjects: mathematics, astronomy, geography, logic, the natural sciences, and theology. He codified the Arab musical scale, still in use today; he also added a fifth string to the *oud* (Arab lute). Many of his works were translated into Latin during the Middle Ages; al-Kindi thus became Alkindus.

Ali's house, near the mosque, is a must-see site. Water from the well of Ali's house is said to possess magical qualities.

Hira

After the fall of Hatra, Hira became the foremost Arab city of Mesopotamia, as well as the Nestorian Christians' base. During its apogee, Hira was ruled by Mudher III (503–554), of the Lakhmid Dynasty. It gets its name from the Syrian *hira*, which means "camp."

After the Islamic conquest, Hira rapidly lost its advantage to Kufa, just a few miles away.

Najaf

Najaf, 63 miles (102 km) from Baghdad, is the fourth holy city of Islam, after Mecca, Medina, and Jerusalem. Muslims worship Ali, the husband of Fatima, Mohammed's daughter, the 4th Caliph and First Imam, who is interred there in a magnificent mausoleum. The cemetery of Najaf is one of the biggest in the world, for Shi'a Muslims do all they can to be buried near the "Prince of Believers."

According to tradition, Ali's body was brought from Kufa and placed following his request on his white camel. Wherever the camel stopped, his people should bury him. The location was kept secret for the duration of the Umayyads' reign.

Other versions say that Ali was buried in the courtyard of the mosque at Kufa, or in Medina, or again transported by his camel all the way to Mazar-e-Sharif in Afghanistan, where another mausoleum stands.

The site of Ali's grave was supposedly found by Caliph Harun al-Rashid during a hunting expedition, thanks to "providential intuition." He immediately ordered a sanctuary to be built upon the newly discovered site. The city of Najaf grew around it. Since then, it has been host to millions of pilgrims.

The mausoleum was burned in the 11th century and rebuilt. The current edifice, dating from 1640, was sacked by Wahabi Arabs in 1802. The great Moroccan traveller, Ibn Batuta, who visited the mausoleum in the early 14th century, recounts that Ali's tomb was raised on a dais, and that the tombs of Adam and Noah were located next to his.

The mosque's dome is covered with 7,777 bricks of pure gold. On the ceiling inside, the names of the imams and a poem in praise of Ali are inscribed in magnificent examples of Arabic calligraphy. One enters the mausoleum through a gate framed by two minarets covered in gold, then passes through gold and silver doors into a square room, with crystalline walls covered with Qur'anic inscriptions. Ali's remains rest in the center of the room, in a coffin of precious wood with ivory inlays, and surrounded by a gold and silver fence.

In the treasury of the sanctuary, the offerings of caliphs, kings, and sultans over the centuries are stored. There is a Qur'an written in the hand of Ali, gold and silver jewels, numerous gems, rugs woven with gold and silk, and even a rice grain upon which an entire Qur'anic sura has been engraved.

Najaf is the most important religious center for Shi'a Muslims. Ayatollah Khomeini lived there as a political refugee from 1965 to 1978.

EIGHT

Karbala and Environs

Karbala is an old name, no doubt of Aramaic origin. It is mentioned by the Prophet Daniel in the Old Testament. Just 60 miles (97 km) from Baghdad, Karbala is most known for the battle that took place there, in which Hussein, the son of Ali and grandson of Mohammed, was ambushed and decapitated. Hussein became a revered martyr for Shi'a Muslims, and Karbala one of their two holiest cities. The gold-leaf cupola and minarets of the sanctuary in which his remains are interred are visible from afar.

In 850, Caliph al-Mutawaqil tried to put a stop to pilgrimages there by destroying the sanctuary built by Caliph al-Ma'mun. A thousand years later, in 1802, the Wahabi shaykh, Saud, invaded Karbala and massacred its inhabitants. He also destroyed Hussein's catafalque and seized the funereal treasures. An immense public outpouring of rage and support brought about a quick restoration of the sanctuary to its former glory.

The mosque is surrounded by a vast courtyard. A wall circling the perimeter is decorated with a blue tile mosaic with Qur'anic calligraphy. There is also a wing with small rooms for clerics and religious students.

Hussein's coffin is enclosed in a silver catafalque about 7 feet high and 12 feet wide. A silver fence protects it from the fervent adorations of pilgrims.

About 300 yards from Hussein's tomb lies that of his half-brother Abbas, revered for having fought at his side. Its dome is also covered in gold leaf, and its main gate is made of silver.

In the cafés that line the street in front of the mosque, clay from

Karbala is sold in briquettes. Shi'a Muslims use them to press against their forehead during prayer; for them, the soil of Karbala is sacred, hallowed by martyrs' blood.

During and after the Iran–Iraq War, pilgrims to Karbala were relatively few. The Iraqi regime is said to have begun to allow Shi'ites to make the pilgrimage again in 1997 (20 years after Saddam Hussein's police forces killed pilgrims on the road to Karbala, and the celebration was outlawed), but US newspaper stories of the jubilant, tense, and widely-reported April 2003 pilgrimage, undertaken after the US bombing of the country and with American protection, contend that the pilgrimage has been outlawed since 1977. In either case, certainly the Shi'ites have been severely repressed under Saddam Hussein's government, and this most visible expression of their faith was long curtailed.

The Battle of Karbala

After the assassination of Ali, Mu'awiya became the 6th Caliph, after forcing Hassan (another of Ali's sons) to abdicate.

Upon Mu'awiya's death in 680, his son Yazid became caliph. But several Muslim chieftains, judging him unworthy of leading the community of believers, refused to recognize his election. Among them was a son of Ali: Hussein, a refugee in Medina.

Hussein let himself be talked into making a bid for the caliphate by Shi'a partisans. They advised him to go to Kufa to ask for help in confronting Yazid. He set out with only 600 men, thirty of whom were companions of the Prophet. They were soon surrounded in the Plain of Karbala.

Caught in a trap, without water for almost a week, Hussein decided to attack. But his troops were vastly outnumbered: on the other side were 4,000 men, commanded by Omar Ibn Saad, son of the victor of the Battle of Qadisiyya.

On October 10, 680, Hussein was beheaded in battle. His head, put in a bag, was presented to Caliph Yazid in Damascus. Today, it rests in the Mosque of al-Hussein in Cairo.

A sanctuary has been built in Damascus on the site where his head was displayed.

The anniversary of the Battle of Karbala and the martyrdom of Hussein is celebrated with great fervor by Shi'a Muslims on the 10th of the month of Moharam. Some have been known to practice self-flagellation and even self-mutilation, expressing their feeling of guilt at having guided Hussein to his death. These practices are forbidden in Iraq.

Lake Razzaza

Visitors may enjoy this complex, about 12 miles (19 km) from Karbala, where you can sail, fish, and swim. To get there, take the old pilgrims' road from Karbala southwest toward Mecca. A fork several miles away gives access, on the right, to Razzaza and the lake of the same name, and also the lake of Habbaniyya further north, returning to Baghdad via Faluja.

If you stay on the road to Mecca, you can see the caves of al-Tar, before coming upon the castle of al-Uqaidir. Shortly before, a road branches off toward the right, toward Ain al-Tamr, located on the other side of Lake Razzaza.

Ain al-Tar

In the middle of the desert, on the road leading to the castle of al-Uqaidir, after Bahr al-Meleh (the salt lake, equivalent of the chotts of North Africa, a vast expanse of stagnant salt water), about 19 miles (30 km) from Karbala, one can see a strange hill—Ain al-Tar. It is pierced with caves, which are inhabited by colonies of bats. According to Japanese archaeologists who studied the site in 1971, people lived in these caves around the second or first centuries BCE. The hill of al-Tar was no doubt a natural fortress, serving to guard the frontier area between the Parthians from the Romans.

Uqaidir

Further along the same road, about 31 miles (50 km) from Karbala, lies the mysterious, fortified palace of al-Uqaidir (the "small oasis"), which thrusts out its imposing walls to all comers in the middle of the desert, near Wadi al-Abyadh (the White Valley). It is probable that a vanished branch of the Euphrates once ran there.

This castle became famous with the 1907 visit of French orientalist Louis Massignon and the spiritual awakening he experienced there.

Al-Uqaidir was built in 778, after the Arab conquest of Iraq, on the foundations of a fortress belonging to the kingdom of Hira. This fortress was the residence of Issa Ibn Moussa, the former wali (governor) of Kufa, who was supposed to become caliph after al-Mansur. But al-Mansur, against the wishes of his father, Abu al-Abbas, founder of the Abbasid dynasty, designated Harun as his successor. Issa Ibn Moussa, forced to renounce the throne, was convinced to content himself with al-Uqaidir, and a considerable financial compensation.

The main entrance of the double-walled fortress faces north. The residential area consisted of three levels. On the ground floor, a huge central hall bisected living quarters. On either side, four identical buildings no doubt housed the harem. The entryway, remarkably set in a series of vaults and arches, faces a mosque, to the right, and the fortress commander's quarters, on the left. An iwan dominates the opposite end of a vast courtyard.

The outer wall, some sixty feet high, was reinforced with regularly spaced towers. Underneath the walkway at the top, a vaulted corridor ran the length of the wall; archers could safely defend the inside as well as the outside of the fort through loopholes along both sides. Boiling oil would be poured on attackers through openings in the wall above the main gate, if they managed to breach the first gate.

Uqaidir Castle was restored in the 1980s.

Ain al-Tamr

The oasis of Ain al-Tamr is situated on the other side of Lake Razzaza, some 81 miles (130 km) west of Karbala. Around 1909, Gertrude Bell had estimated the number of palm trees at 170,000. Many Baghdadis spent the weekend there with their families, in the time of year just before it gets too hot to travel. The oasis is famous for its pleasant climate, its mineral water, and its dates. It is known to all Arabs as the birthplace of the famous general, Mussa Ibn Nasair, who conquered Spain.

Once called Shethatha, Ain al-Tamr came into its own around the first and second centuries CE. Shapur I, the Persian king, is said to have held his wedding at Ain al-Tamr, when he married Princess Nadira, daughter of the king of Hatra, after Nadira had helped him conquer the city. Under the Abbasids, the oasis became a major stopping point of the caravan trade.

— NINE —

Abraham: Prophet and Iraqi

"Abraham was neither a Jew nor a Christian, but he was a true believer and servant of God."
—*The Qur'an*

Until the 20th century, when archeologists began exploring its hidden treasures, the city of Ur had been untouched since its destruction for several millennia, buried under a huge mound of earth. Today, from the top of the restored ziggurat of Ur, one enjoys an uninterrupted view of the Chaldean desert. The network of irrigation canals has disappeared, and the Euphrates has changed its course, far from where it quenched the thirst of the ancient inhabitants of Ur.

The site of Ur was located in 1853, when the British vice-consul of Basra, exploring a hill that the bedouins called al-Mougheir (Tar Hill), found clay cylinders inscribed with the name of Nabonid, a king of Ur from the 6th century. The last king of Babylon, somewhat of an archeologist, had rebuilt the ancient ziggurat, and he wished to remind posterity that it had been built by Ur-Nammu and his son Dungi, "kings of Ur, kings of Sumer and of Akkad, kings of the four regions of the earth," who reigned in 2300 BCE.

Looking north from the top of the ziggurat, one can see the Euphrates River, about 10 miles (16 km) away, winding through a verdant area before Nasiriya. Toward the south, only a few hundred yards from the tower, there is a vast open pit of ruins. You can descend into it by way of a rickety wooden stairway, all the way to the "Well of the Dead," where the British archeologist, Leonard Wooley, discovered the tomb of Queen Shubad, buried 6,500 years ago with her retinue. Nearby, he found a golden helmet and a sword made of electrum belonging to Meskalamdug, "Hero of the Divine Earth." Today, there are more bats and snakes than valuable artifacts. But this is the place where Wooley was certain that Abraham had lived, in a house of unbaked bricks, 4,000 years ago, before leaving Mesopotamia for the "land of Canaan," or Palestine.

Noah of Sumer

While the wanderings of Abraham are amply recounted in the Old Testament and the Qur'an, little is known about his life in Chaldea. Legends abound, though, in the Midrash (Jewish rabbinical writings) and in the writings of Muslim authors such as al-Tabari.

Abraham was not yet born, said the ancient chroniclers, but his father Terah (Azar in the Qur'an) was already an important personality in Ur. He was a direct descendant of Noah, the legendary hero who had survived the flood, and whom the Sumerians called Zisudra. The Sumerians sang his memory in the Epic of Gilgamesh, the hero-king of Uruk who had met Noah and received from him the secret of eternal life. On clay tablets placed some centuries later in the Ashurbanipal library at Nineveh (668–667 BCE), his name was Utnaphistim. He would become Noah by the time of the writing of Genesis.

The skepticism prevalent at the beginning of the 20th century about the Biblical flood was dissipated when Wooley discovered traces of its damage at the bottom of a well dug in Ur (see Chapter 12). Of course, finding the Ark is a much more difficult task! At Najaf, where Mohammad's son-in-law Ali is buried, there is an excavation purported to have revealed the site where the Ark was built. Ibn Batuta, the 14th-century Moroccan voyager, visited Najaf and wrote of a mausoleum said to be Noah's. His coffin was exposed on a gold-plated platform.

Today, research at Mount Ararat (where Noah's Ark came to rest, according to the Bible) in eastern Turkey has remained inconclusive. Some say the Ark probably never left Mesopotamia. The elements would have swept it toward the hill country of Kurdistan, near Sulaimaniya.

The ruins of Abraham's house in Ur

Nimrud, "Great Hunter of the Eternal"

Like Sargon and Moses, Nimrud was "given to the River" at birth. But in his case, his mother, who believed he was a devil, wanted to drown him. Nimrud was saved and raised by a panther. Once grown, he revealed his gifts as a leader of men. Having taken the city of Kuta-Rabah, he proclaimed himself King of Ur. He chose a certain Terah, one of Noah's descendants, as his vizier and confidante.

But power went to the young king's head. He declared himself to be a divine incarnation, and had statues made in his image for people to worship. His vizier became rich by setting up shop making and selling thousands of these idols to the populace.

Highly superstitious, Nimrud lived surrounded by astrologers, seers, and all kinds of *magi*. Like many kings of his time, he had his dreams interpreted. One day, while he was napping, a voice came to him and said, "Woe be to those who do not recognize the God of Abraham! Truth comes out one day, and lies disappear!" Then the king saw all his idols crashing to the ground. Upon awakening, Nimrud immediately called his astrologers. They told him that a child, Abraham, would be born, who would grow up to overthrow him, and challenge the Mesopotamian religion. The only solution, the astrologers said, was to eliminate all male newborns.

The decree was applied until Amatlai, Terah's wife, became pregnant. She was convinced it was going to be a boy. Fearing for his life, she hid her pregnancy, and delivered her child "in a cave." This place, if it exists, has never been found in the entire region of Ur; the country is so flat that there are no caves. Another legend says that Amatlai took refuge on one of the islands of the swamp region near the mouth of the Euphrates. It is more plausibly surmised that she had stayed for some time at Borsippa (today called Birs-Nimrud), a city near Babylon. In Borsippa, on a hill near the ruins of the ziggurat, there is a much-frequented sanctuary. In fact, it was built over a cave where Abraham was supposedly born. Pilgrims can easily descend a steep staircase to the bottom. In a small "room," they sit on prayer rugs disposed on the floor, facing a wall, and a plaque with a sura from the Qur'an celebrating the "Friend of God." The entrance to the sacred cave is walled in, and protected with bars made of silver.

Abraham's Youth

Abraham had a healthy, uneventful childhood, thanks to the protection of the Archangel Gabriel. Years passed, and Amatlai ended up revealing to her husband that he was the father of a boy, and that they couldn't go on hiding him. Terah was furious, and at a loss as to how to save his son. Of course, thirteen years had passed since the dream, but he had no idea how the king would react. Finally, he decided that the only solution was to tell Nimrud the truth, and to convince him that this child was not the one designated in the prophecy. Meanwhile, he named his son Abram (only much later, in Palestine, would he be called Abraham).

Awaiting his audience with the King, Terah surely had no idea that his son, though but a boy, had already attained an uncommon state of spiritual awareness. Indeed, he was already persuaded that the movements of the stars and planets could have no other cause than a

Supreme Being, and that this God could only be unique and master of all things.

Nimrud was not pleased, but realized he could not just have the 13-year-old Abraham executed. He tried, in vain, to have him imprisoned. In a last attempt to escape fate, he moved the capital to Babylon and called himself Hammurabi. He had taken care to bring Terah with him, and forbidden Abraham from leaving Ur.

Today, the ruins of Babylon, situated about 62 miles (100 km) from Baghdad, are not those of the city Hammurabi built, but those of the Babylon of Nabuchadnezzar II (605–562 BCE). Abraham's Babylon was demolished by invaders, then razed by the Syrian king, Sennacherib, in 689 BCE. Today, evidence of the site of Hammurabi's famous Tower of Babylon is better seen from the air.

The Burning Furnace

Abraham took advantage of his "house arrest" at Ur to educate himself. But he soon became bored and eager to confront Nimrud. God was ordering him to go to Babylon. At the time, the road was a dangerous one, infested with bandits and lions. But, carried on the Archangel Gabriel's wings, Abraham made the trip in a day.

For those unassisted by angels, the road follows the Euphrates, passing by the sites of Larsa and Uruk, then turns north, cutting across a wide stretch of monotonous desert until Diwaniya. The landscape then becomes marshier, with interspersed saltpans. Women dressed in black, barefoot, gather the salt and pile it up in mounds, carrying it off in bags to sell to a nearby factory. Approaching Babylon, the landscape becomes cultivated fields dotted with palm trees.

Upon arriving in Babylon, Abraham found his family, and the young Sarah who would become his wife. He began to preach his faith in one God, "God of the Heavens, God of Gods, God of Nimrud," hoping to convince the king to abandon idol worship.

But it was not easy for Abraham to spread the word of his faith in the great city of Babylon. As was to be expected, Nimrud did not listen to the young man from Ur. One day, Abraham had an idea. He took a hatchet and shattered all the idols in his father's shop, except for the biggest among them. When Terah returned, Abraham explained that he had placed an offering at the foot of the statue, but that the idols had fought over it and destroyed each other. He pointed to the one intact idol, from India, and said to his father, "Ask her. Maybe she can talk."

"What do you mean?" replied Terah. "You know very well that they have no awareness of what goes on." Upon which Abraham answered, "How is it then, father, that your ears hear not what your mouth says?"

Terah's convictions were shaken, but he dared not disown them completely. Babylon was outraged by Abraham's sacrilege, and the people demanded that he be thrown into a burning furnace. Nimrud had him imprisoned, and left him without food for forty days. A huge bonfire was lit. The Patriarch, who had not starved to death, was placed in a catapult and thrown into the blaze.

According to legend, Abraham faced this torture without flinching, refusing even the Archangel's help. Before a stupefied populace, the flames would not burn his body. The fire was cold. A spring welled out of the ground nearby. It was a miracle, an undeniable sign of the power of Abraham's God. On that day, many Babylonians converted and shattered their idols.

After this Terah and his family thought it best to return to Ur. Abraham married Sarah. But the city had changed. During their absence Ur's inhabitants had neglected the former capital, tired of fighting against the encroaching desert, which was gradually swallowing up the delta. Terah made the decision to emigrate to Canaan with his family. In a small caravan, they followed the Euphrates to Harran, an important Mesopotamian commercial and religious center whose vestiges are in southern Turkey.

Abraham, his wife, and his father remained longer than planned in Harran. Terah was in the company of fellow believers in the Moon-god called Sin. Abraham preached, and won converts. He spent his nights studying the heavens and dreaming of the child Sarah would soon bear. But time passed; his father died, and few ties bound him any longer to the region. One night under a starry sky, as he wondered how he was going to respond to the pleas of citizens of Ur for his return, he heard a voice within, urging him on to Canaan.

Exile in Palestine was to be God's second test. Abraham left Mesopotamia without looking back, but he would always remain nostalgic for his birthplace and the civilization of his ancestors.

Abraham, Mandean Prophet

Jews, Muslims, and Christians are not the only peoples to consider Abraham a prophet. The Mandeans too hold Abraham very dear, although their primary saint is John the Baptist. They say that Abraham was their first baptizer, and that he left Ur for Harran and Palestine because he was rejected by his community because of his circumcision (see Chapter 5).

The Mandeans say that they emigrated with Abraham to the River Jordan, their sacred river, until the execution of John the Baptist and the Christ. They then returned to the delta region in southern Mesopotamia, reproaching Jesus for having co-opted the baptismal rite and founded a new religion.

Ur, City of the Aryans

A contemporary translator of the Qur'an, Hamidullah, thinks that the personality of Abraham and the events of his life inspired the Indian *Ramayana*, the Sanskrit poem that recounts the exploits of Prince Rama.

Rama is an incarnation of the supreme god, Vishnu, who came to earth to restore peace and justice. He represents the ancient ideal of the Aryans, an Indo-European nomadic people that invaded Punjab around 1500 BCE and founded Indian civilization.

This historian reminds us that the Aryans had settled in Iraq and Iran before continuing their way toward India around the time of Abraham. According to Hamidullah, the word "Aryan" comes from the city of Ur, where they must have lived very long ago.

The Ramayana was composed in the first millenium BCE by the poet, Valmiki, who drew upon a legend brought back from Iraq by Aryan travellers. This theory is impossible to verify, but it is true that there are many analogies in both stories, to begin with, the names Rama and Ab-Ram. As for relations between India and Mesopotamia, they go back very far. People have searched for a long time the site of the famous Dilmun, the paradise where Noah/Zisudra retired in the Gilgamesh epic. The latest consensus is that it is Bahrain. Archaeological vestiges discovered on the island, which is situated in the Gulf about halfway to the Strait of Oman, attest to its role as a bridge between Mesopotamia and India.

Samuel Kramer, a Mesopotamia expert, goes even further, affirming that Noah stopped in Bahrain, but only stayed there a short while. He then returned to the country of his ancestors, at the mouth of the Indus River.

Polemic around the Patriarch

The ambiguities abundant in the Old Testament have brought grist to the mills of those historians who deny the existence of Abraham. They find it strange that the names of the Patriarch, and of his enemy Nimrud, have been found on none of the thousands of clay tablets recovered in Iraq.

Yet archaeological research in Mesopotamia has corroborated Biblical writings. The tablets that have been unearthed and those that still sleep in the sand have not yet yielded all their secrets. Some years ago the name of a certain Ab-ra-mu was deciphered on a tablet found in Ebla, in Syria. Researchers at the site deduced that Abraham was not from Chaldea, but from the "country of Sham." Archeologists even found a city in the region that was called Ur in the early third millenium BCE. The debate opened by these discoveries and interpretations is not close to being resolved.

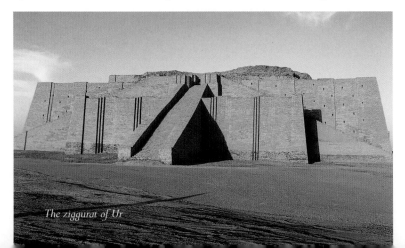

The ziggurat of Ur

TEN

From Baghdad to Basra
(via Kut)

Kut

The city of Kut extends along the banks of the Tigris where it meets the canal of al-Gharraf, which connects the Tigris with Nasiriya and the al-Shuyukh Souk on the Euphrates, 99 miles (160 km) southeast of Baghdad.

Kut became an important city when the British river navigation Lynch Company set up operations in Basra with the aim of establishing a line to Baghdad. During World War I, the British expeditionary corps, led by General Townshend, suffered a crushing defeat at the hands of the German-backed Ottoman Army. The city was laid to siege, and thousands of troops perished or were wounded before the ultimate British surrender. Not yet a colonel, T.E. Lawrence had been sent to Kut from the Cairo British intelligence bureau with the mission of buying the support of a Turkish General, Khalil Pasha. He was not successful.

Wasit

This once-legendary city is now in ruins. Formerly the Umayyad capital, it gives its name to one of Iraq's governorates. Situated along the Kut al-Hay, 25 miles (40 km) southeast of Kut, it lies within one of the ancient riverbeds of the Tigris.

Wasit was built from the ground up by Governor Hajaj, who thought the Iraqi people undisciplined, especially in Kufa and Basra, the two biggest cities at the time. He moved into the new city around 706, protected by Syrian troops. Hajaj chose the name "Wasit," which means "the middle," for its strategic placement halfway between the two unruly cities.

The city lost its dominant position under the Abbasids. Like Hajaj, they too left Kufa for security reasons, to build a new capital: Baghdad. In the 15th century, the Tigris progressively changed course away from Wasit, ending the fortunes of the city.

A Treasure Buried in the Mud of the Shatt al-Arab

In 1856, a convoy of six *keleks* (rafts made of inflated bags of animal skin) carrying unusual cargo was attacked by bandits north of Kurna, a village situated not far from the delta of the Tigris and the Euphrates, on the Shatt al-Arab River.

The convoy was carrying a series of monumental statues and reliefs in marble and bronze, which had been taken from the ruins of Khorsabad, Assyria's capital under Sargon II. (A few years earlier, the site had been discovered by Paul Emile Botta and Victor Place, two French consular agents posted in Mosul.) Some of these statues, such as the winged bulls that guarded the gates of the palace, weighed over 32 tons.

Not surprisingly, four of the six *keleks* sank. The statues that could be saved were shipped to Paris, where they can be seen today at the Louvre. Unfortunately, most of the pieces are still at the bottom of the Shatt al-Arab.

The first attempt to recover this buried treasure never materialized; in 1856, the technology available was insufficient to raise such heavy and voluminous objects.

One hundred years later, Pierre de Vaucelles came across a map indicating the site of the wreck in the French Chancellery. The French Ambassador resolved to pursue the affair with the Iraqi Directorate of Antiquities. He asked the famous oceanologist, Jacques-Yves Cousteau, to participate in the operation. The project was abandoned before it was even launched, though, when diplomatic relations between France and Iraq soured following the Suez Canal crisis.

Another equally ill fated recovery attempt was made in the 1960s. The Japanese mission led by an imperial prince discovered that, after a century, the course of the Shatt al-Arab River had changed. Since then, the ancient treasure has remained buried under tons of silt.

Amara

Amara grew up around a Turkish fort built in 1862 on the left bank of the Tigris, to watch over the tribes of the area. The city benefited from the river traffic generated by the Basra–Baghdad line, which was inaugurated at the end of the 19th century.

The swampy landscape here extends all the way to the Iranian border, barely 31 miles (50 km) away. The soil is highly fertile, yielding plentiful harvests of rice and wheat.

Kurna

Kurna stands on the site of the former city of Digha. Its strategic importance grew when the Euphrates changed course to join the Tigris, creating the Shatt al-Arab.

The Tree of Adam and Eve

The Tree of Adam and Eve

At the confluence of the Euphrates and the Tigris, about 46 miles (74 km) going toward Baghdad from Basra, the "Tree of Adam and Eve" has long attracted visitors. It is said to have been planted by Noah after the Flood at the exact spot where a similar tree had stood in the middle of the Garden of Eden.

This sacred tree, whose infamous fruit God (according to the Old Testament) had forbidden to Adam and Eve, almost provoked a general revolt of the Arab tribes of the region during the British invasion of Iraq at the beginning of World War I. After a British soldier broke off a branch of the tree as a good-luck charm, General Townshend, commander of the expeditionary corps, was forced to publicly discipline the iconoclastic trooper to avoid a crisis.

The Turks had built a fort there in the 16th century, augmenting it with a military base against the Persians. Kurna was occupied by the British in December 1914.

The Tomb of Ezra

The prophet Ezra is buried at the confluence of the two rivers. His tomb drew many Jewish pilgrims, who took the Lynch Company's steamboats from Basra to Baghdad in the early 20th century.

Ezra, or al-Uzayr (457–432 BCE) was one of the great reformers of the Torah. The Qur'an reproaches the Hebrews for considering him to be a "Son of God." According to al-Tabari, the author of *Stories of the Prophets*, this epithet was given to him because he had succeeded in reconstituting portions of the text of the Law that had been forgotten by the Hebrews—whom God had punished for not respecting the precepts contained therein. The Torah purportedly descended from the heavens in the form of a flame that pierced the Prophet's heart.

The Swamplands: People of the Marshes

The swamp region, an area of wetlands covered with reeds and palm trees, extends from the mouth of the Tigris and the Euphrates up through Nasiriya, Khurna, Kubaish, and Amara.

The local population lives on artificial islands built of reeds, palm thatch, and mud. The houses are built of reed and cane, and supported on thick trunks of *qassab*, a sort of giant bamboo. Every swamp village has its *moudhif*, or guesthouse.

Outside of the main arteries of navigation, the people of the swamps are the only ones who can find their way in the shifting labyrinth of channels. They move about in flat boats called *tarada*, made of reeds, tightly bound and covered over in tar and petroleum. They cultivate rice, practice spearfishing and hunt for wild boar, dangerous animals that damage crops. The fauna is mostly winged: ducks and coots, gray and white Siberian geese, pelicans (whose pouched beaks are prized as drumskins). But there are also the ever-present black water buffalo, which are like members of the family. Their dried manure serves as a fuel.

Since the beginning of historical times, the swamplands have always been a refuge for rebels. The best known was the Zang, a band of black slaves chased by the Abbasid authorities in the late 9th century (see page 146). According to legend, an island called Hufaidh in the middle of the swamp, covered with orchards and palaces, is guarded by jinn, mischievous demons who hide the island from the view of humans.

Since the construction of the Saddam Canal, which was built, according to the Iraqi government, to regulate the flow of the Tigris and Euphrates and to wash away the excessively salty waters of the Shatt al-Arab, an estimated 93 percent of the swamplands has been drained. Naturally, this has forced the peoples of the swamps to abandon their traditional way of life. Human Rights Watch has called the water diversion plan and its decastating impact on the Marsh Arabs, a "crime against humanity."

Life in the once-flourishing swamplands

The Zang Slaves' Revolt

In the 9th century, Southern Iraq reeled with one of the most important known slave revolts of antiquity, ranking with that of Spartacus.

African slaves worked by the thousands on farms and construction sites in the Shatt al-Arab area, in especially squalid conditions. They were called the Zang, for many came from Zanzibar and the coast of East Africa. Their miserable living conditions caused regular uprisings, in a terrain perfect for guerilla warfare. In the Maysan area, the swamp is particularly dense, entirely covered over with reeds, and criss-crossed with canals.

Ali Ben Mohammad, chief of the slave revolt, was an Arab born on the Persian border. Highly intelligent, well versed in astrology and witchcraft, he was the official poet at the court of Caliph al-Muntasir, at Samara. In 863 he moved to Bahrain. An ambitious man and a great orator, he went around proclaiming himself a descendant of Ali, or even a prophet.

His first attempt at revolution failed. The bedouins that he had convinced to participate in overthrowing the Caliph were brutally defeated.

After taking refuge in Baghdad, Ali claimed to possess supernatural powers, notably that of reading the minds of his disciples. Learning about unrest in Basra, he went to the edge of the swampland, and sent agitators in to incite the slaves to revolt.

In 869, during a huge meeting, he promised the Zang to improve their living conditions, make them rich, and never betray them. Their revolt would shake the whole region.

The Zang rebels were soon in the tens of thousands. Wasit and Basra were pillaged and their inhabitants massacred. Backed by bedouins who had come to join their fight, they severely disturbed the pilgrimage to Mecca by destabilizing the region. They nearly succeeded in forming an alliance with the Karmats, who were also in revolt against the central authorities, but failed at the last minute.

The Zang were finally vanquished by Abu Abbas in 883. When they saw the head of their chief impaled on a spear, Ali Ben Mohammad's partisans surrendered en masse. The leaders of the revolt were crucified, but still it took almost three years for things to stabilize. Many Zang rebels also hid in the swamplands, where they took up banditry.

ELEVEN

Basra: Venice of the Orient

Basra

Basra is known all over the world as the port where Sinbad set sail on his fabulous voyages. Between Zubayr and Basra, you can see "the Tower of Sinbad," one of the rare vestiges of the legendary port.

Basra was built on a network of canals, which gives it a distinctly Venetian look. The site was occupied by the Greeks, who founded the villages of Ditiridis and Teredon, then by the Sassanids, who called the town Vahishtabad. The quarter of Ashar occupies the former site of the Roman town of Apologos. Basra was founded in 637 by Otba bin Ghazwan, a companion of the Prophet and military commander under Caliph Omar. His troops, preparing to conquer the rest of Iraq and Persia, were camped near a place that the bedouins called al-Kharayba, meaning "the ruin," probably one of the vanished villages. This site is situated west of present-day Basra, at Zubayr.

Zubayr bears the name of another of the Prophet's companions, the fifth to convert to Islam. Mohammad had promised him Paradise, and called him al-Hawari (the Apostle). He died in the famous Battle of the Camels, in 656.

In the 8th century, Basra's population was 300,000. It was a prosperous commercial and financial center, thanks to its port and its export products, such as dates. Basra boasted over 500 different types of dates, of world-renowned quality.

Basra is, according to the French historian Louis Massignon, the "veritable crucible where Muslim civilization took shape." Indeed, during the Abbasid epoch, Basra's intelligentsia rivaled that of Baghdad. Arabic grammar was first codified in Basra. The school of

Hassan al-Basri (died in 728) had a considerable influence on Islamic thought, in particular its more mystic currents. He left no writings, but is often quoted, his sayings becoming part of Islam's vast oral tradition. He is known for having said, "The world is a bridge that you cross, but upon which you should build nothing."

Basra was pillaged by the Qarmats in 923, then destroyed by the Mongols in 1258. In the 17th century, under Ottoman rule, enterprising local officials opened Basra to British, Portuguese, and Dutch merchants.

The first missions and trading company offices set up operations in the 19th century. In 1850, Basra became the administrative seat of the *vilayat* that included what is now Kuwait.

The first great battle opposing the Turks and the British expeditionary corps occurred on April 14, 1915. After a brutal firefight against the troops led by General Sir Arthur Barrett at Shaiba, west of Basra, the Turks beat a retreat. One thousand men died under the command of General Sir John Nixon, victorious against the Turkish general, Sulaiman al-Askari, who committed suicide.

Today, the dead of a more recent war are commemorated in a series of monumental statues of Iraqi generals who died fighting Iran in the 1980s, along the Shatt al-Arab. The statues all face Iran.

Above: Houses along one of Basra's many canals

The Battle of the Camel

As soon as he took power, Caliph Ali had to deal with revolt from every quarter. Aisha, Mohammed's widow, had opposed his election. Two of the Prophet's Companions, Zubayr and Talha, backed her protest. With their partisans, they took Basra.

Ali, with his faithful batallion of soldiers from Kufa, marched on the city successfully, in a battle named for the camel upon which Aisha, at the center of the melee, rode.

Basra's climate is not a very healthy one: in the summer, high humidity makes the heat unbearable.

Pillaged Museum

During the first Gulf War (1991), the Hague Convention of 1954, which protects "cultural treasures in case of war," was not respected. The al-Makhal mosque was destroyed and the al-Khawaz mosque damaged. The museum was also pillaged: heads taken from statues, and artworks and old manuscripts stolen. Certain rare pieces appeared on the international art market in 1992, in the United States and in Switzerland.

The Mausoleum of Zubayr

Zubayr, a cousin of Mohammed, was the fifth of the Prophet's companions to convert to Islam. He was given the supreme honor of leading the wake upon Mohammed's death. His mausoleum is at Zubayr, near Basra.

Below: Basra, 1950: the banks of the Euphrates (photo © Roland Bareilles)

The Revolt of the Qarmats

The Qarmats are disciples of Hamdan Qarmat, "the red-eyed one," a revolutionary from Kufa who in 890 promised social justice and redistribution of wealth. For almost a century, the Qarmats led a series of popular revolts.

Hamdan abandoned his political activity early on, but his revolutionary ideas had already spread. One of his followers declared an independent state in the oasis of al-Hasa in Arabia. Another was executed in 903 after a failed bid for the Caliphate. The Qarmats' most important success was taking the island of Bahrain in the 10th century.

Their chief in this adventure was Abu Tahir, who put forth the opinion that the conjunction of Jupiter and Saturn in the year 928 was the sign of the coming of the Mahdi (the Qur'anic messiah, supposed to appear at the end of time), the fall of Islam, and the beginning of a new, last religious era.

The Bahraini Qarmats sacked Basra and Kufa, and in 927, Abu Tahir made a vain attempt to take Baghdad. The exploit for which he is most reviled by Muslims was the taking of Mecca in 930. He and his followers committed atrocities and massacres at a time of year when pilgrims were most numerous in the Muslim holy city, and stole the sacred black rock, the Qa'aba.

In October 931, Abu Tahir, convinced that the 1,500th anniversary of the death of Zoroaster heralded the beginning of a new era, designated a young Persian, in whom he saw the future Mahdi, as his successor. Actually, the man was a dangerous lunatic. He ordered the Qarmats to curse all the prophets and to worship fire, and had several Qarmat leaders executed. Abu Tahir regained control and had the Persian killed 80 days later. Many sect members were demoralized by this episode, and left Bahrain to join the Caliph's army.

After Abu Tahir's death in 944, his brothers succeeded him at the head of the Qarmat movement, and returned the Qa'aba to Mecca in 941. They had the stone thrown into the Friday mosque at Kufa with the following message attached: "We were ordered to take it; we were ordered to give it back." In fact, the third Fatimid caliph, al-Mansur, asked them to return it, and explained that the ground would refuse to receive the body of Ubayd Allah, a high official who had died in North Africa, as long as the Qa'aba was not restored to its rightful place.

The great stone, according to the engineer recruited by King Faisal of Arabia to rebuild the Great Mosque at Mecca, had been broken into seven pieces. This was interpreted in various ways by the Qarmats, as a reference to the seven imams venerated by certain Shi'ites, or to the seven imams who are to lead the world during the final religious era, or to the seven continents, and so forth.

Mirbad

Mirbad is a small town near Basra where caravans used to regroup. Until the 13th century, poets went there to recite their works, in contests that had a profound influence on Arab literature.

In 1970, the Iraqi government decided to revive this tradition. A festival was organized in Basra in memory of ancient Mirbad. It is mainly for Arab poets, though many foreign writers and poets have been invited. The festival moved to Baghdad in 1985 for reasons of convenience. The poetry competitions are broadcast live on TV and radio.

Fao

This deep-water port is situated at the mouth of the Shatt al-Arab, south of Basra. Its importance is a direct function of its strategic location. Fao was the beachhead for British invasion troops during World War I. The Poona Division debarked in November 1914, after secretly quitting Bombay. Sir Arthur Barrett's expeditionary force of 15,000 men took Basra on November 22. It was also the theater of one of the major, and final, battles of the Iran–Iraq War.

War torn Fao

—— TWELVE ——

From Najaf to Basra

The road from Najaf to Basra follows the west bank of the Euphrates going toward Samawa, Nasiriya, and Souk al-Shuyukh. The great archeological sites of Sumer and Akkad are arrayed on both sides of the river.

To visit Nippur, Uruk, Lagash, and Larsa, one must cross the river. Turn left a few miles from Najaf going toward Diwaniya. To go to Nippur and Lagash, cross the Diwaniya River near Kut.

Uruk and Larsa are on the east bank of the Euphrates, further south, near Nasiriya. Ur, Eridu, and al-Obeid are also situated in the environs of Nasiriya, on the west bank of the Euphrates.

Nippur

In the fourth millenium BCE, Nippur was the main religious center of Mesopotamia. The sanctuary at Nippur was devoted to one of the most important gods of the Sumerian pantheon, Enlil, "Lord of the Spirit Wind," who decides the fates of men. When the gods met to decide whether or not to curse humanity with the Deluge, it was Enlil who had the final say. During the Babylonian period, the city ceased to play its important religious role.

Today, almost nothing remains of Nippur's ziggurat, also known as the Wind Mountain. The fortress that either the Seleucids or the Parthians built on top of the site is in ruins.

An American archaeologist digging in Nippur at the end of the 19th century found several thousand clay tablets dating from Sumerian times, including tablets relating the story of the Flood.

Samawa

This small city on the lower Euphrates benefited from its strategic location and its role as a communications hub for river traffic. Samawa was twice pillaged by Wahabi Arabs during campaigns against Najaf in the early 19th century.

Uruk (Warka)

"I am the one called Gilgamesh. I am the Pilgrim of all the roads in the country and all the roads outside the country. I am the one to whom all has been revealed, hidden truths, the mysteries of life and above all, of death. I have known Inanna in the bed of Holy Marriage, I have crushed demons and conversed with the gods. I am two-thirds god, and one-third man."

Twelve miles (20 km) from where the Euphrates now flows, near Khidr, one can find the ancient site of Uruk, called Erek in Genesis.

The Lords of Uruk are almost all mythical heroes. King Lugalbanda set out in search of the "Tablets of Destiny" stolen by the tempest-god, Zu. King Dumuzi descended into hell, in love with the goddess Ishtar. But the best known is certainly king Gilgamesh, who is supposed to have reigned in the 27th century BCE. The epic in which he is the central figure foreshadows Homer's *Odyssey*, and the legends of the Holy Grail.

Gilgamesh looked for, and found Utnapishtim (Zisudra in Sumerian), owner of the secret of immortality. Utnapishtim told him the story of the Flood, and gave him a plant possessing the virtue of Youth. A serpent later stole this precious plant while Gilgamesh slept.

The ruins of the sacred perimeter devoted to Inanna, goddess of fertility, only hint at what must have been an impressive temple. One of the more original sites is that of the "White Temple," built in the early third millenium BCE on a hill, before the time of ziggurats. A sculpted marble head discovered at Uruk, called the "Lady of Warka," is a masterpiece, and powerfully conveys the degree of civilization achieved by Sumer.

The ruins of Uruk disappeared during the Abbasid epoch, buried in the swamps of the Tigris and Euphrates. They only reappeared in the

Harvesting salt on the Euphrates floodplain

16th century, when the Tigris recovered its former course, some distance away from the ruins.

In 1967, a German archaeological mission discovered the ruins of three square walls, each 30 yards long. At the center, a sort of lid seemed to cover the entrance to a tomb. In fact, this was supposed to be the entrance to the netherworld. Legend recounts that the goddess Inanna, wife of the god Tammuz, had entered the building. As she walked to the center of the courtyard, her clothes and jewels were removed one by one. It is said that the goddess's sister killed her with her stare, and that the inanimate body of Inanna was introduced into the vault. This tragic legend is a precursor of Greek tragedy, especially of the plays of Aeschylus.

Larsa (Senkereh)

A dozen miles (20 km) southwest of Uruk, Larsa is the site of ruins of a ziggurat and of the Temple of the Rising Sun, devoted to the sun god Shamash, or Utu in Sumerian.

Founded in the third millenium BCE by an Amorite conqueror from Syria, Larsa reached its apogee around the 19th–18th centuries BCE, only to fall under Babylonian influence in Hammurabi's time.

The site was excavated in 1933 by the French archaeologist, André Parrot. He unearthed numerous objects in the ruins of houses; a vase from this expedition now rests in the Louvre. The French evacuation house was destroyed in the 1991 war, and the site's guard was murdered. In 2003, the site had been looted, and no guard was on the site, where many clay tablets with cuneiform texts have been discovered.

Nasiriya

Nasiriya was established in 1870, on the east bank of the Euphrates, by Muntafiq, Shaykh of the confederation of Arab tribes.

The Turks had taken care to plan a rectilinear grid of streets, the better to control the city in case of revolts.

The city's souk is especially vibrant, and it is very pleasant to walk along the riverbank in the evening. One passes the façade of a Mandean temple. The remains of a bridge crossing the Euphrates remind us that one of the most devastating battles of the first Gulf War took place in the Nasiriya area.

Not surprisingly, given its strategic location along the way from Basra to Baghdad, the city again saw action during the 2003 American/British invasion, and the US Marines camped in the city's museum.

Al-Shuyukh Souk

The city is situated on the west bank of the Euphrates, in a rather unhealthy, swampy area. It was founded in the 18th century by the chief of the Muntafiq tribes around a mosque and souk where they would congregate. *Shuyukh* is the plural of shaykh.

Lagash (Tello)

The site of Lagash, about 56 miles (90 km) from Nasiriya, has turned out to be a veritable mine of historical treasures, for archaeologists—and for thieves, too. Several French archaeological teams carried out extensive digs at the site: Henri de Sarzac (1877–1900), Gaston Gros (1903–1909), Henri de Genouillac (1929–1931), and finally André Parrot (1931–1933).

Lagash was founded in the fourth millennium. Among the various dynasties to hold power in the city, Ur-Nanshe, whose best-known sovereign is Eanatum, reached its prime around 2580 BCE. A stela has been found, called the "Stela of Vultures," which commemorates Eanatum's victory over the city-state of Uma. It is on display in the Louvre.

Sargon of Akkad's funeral mask

Around the second half of the 22nd century BCE, under the reign of Patesi Goudea (head of state and high priest), the sculptural art of the Sumerians was at its height. For André Parrot, the inscriptions and reliefs discovered at Lagash and now at the Louvre contain numerous analogies to Biblical writings.

Ur

The beginnings of Ur are lost in pre-history. A cluster of mud huts, no doubt, perched on an island amid the swamps of Mesopotamia.

Now, the ruins of a house claimed to be that of the patriarch Abraham are the most visited in Ur (for more on Abraham, see Chapter 9).

For countless years, travellers were intrigued by a huge mound located near al-Muqayyar. At its foot, bedouins had grazed their sheep for millennia. No one however imagined the great hill to contain the ziggurat of Ur, until 1853, when the British vice-consul at Basra found the signature cylinder deep in the mound. The edifice buried there was indeed a great ziggurat.

Situated on the west bank of the Euphrates about 6 miles (10 km) from Nasiriya, Ur, the Biblical city of the Chaldeans and the surmised birthplace of Abraham, has surely given up only a small portion of its secrets.

Woolley's Archeological Finds

During the British occupation of Mesopotamia, the archaeological digs at Ur were headed by Leonard Woolley, who in 1927 discovered a massive flagstone floor. Since this was a rarity, Woolley dug it up, and found a huge space that looked like a royal tomb. Further excavations revealed something extraordinary: a ramp leading to another tomb. Soon, Woolley came upon skeletons of men wearing swords, and female skeletons with jeweled headdresses. Still further, Woolley found a chariot decorated with mosaics, with its team of donkeys and drivers. At the end of the deep vault, Woolley came upon a big wooden box, in poor shape. Moving it revealed a hole where thieves had broken into the tomb. On the other side, there was another tomb. The objects that accompanied the buried king had disappeared.

Woolley and his team went on to find another set of tombs, with the same macabre group of guardians. In one of them, Queen Shubad, who lived some 5,000 years ago rested in a coffin filled with the pearls of gold and silver that must have decorated her robes. A lapis-lazuli cylinder inscribed with her name identified the queen. Around her were at least 25 skeletons, of soldiers, but also of ladies-in-waiting, as well as a treasure trove of precious artifacts: bowls and golden lamps, copperware and jewels.

In contrast, the tomb of Meskalamdug, the "Prince of the Good

Country" who lived around 2500 BCE, bore no evidence of collective human sacrifice. He was accompanied in death only by his personal effects: golden daggers and other weapons, such as an axe made of electrum (an alloy of gold and silver), platters inscribed with his name, some jewels and a massive gold helmet, one of the most beautiful ever discovered in Mesopotamia.

While digging at Ur, Leonard Woolley made yet another sensational discovery: evidence of the Flood, or at least of a flood of catastrophic proportions. More than 40 feet underground, beneath the royal tombs, he hit a layer of clay over eight feet thick. This huge accumulation of silt bore witness to the destructive force unleashed upon an entire civilization by the rising waters. The history of Mesopotamia is indeed made of upheavals, both human and natural.

In 1930–31, Woolley unearthed the tombs of the kings Dungi and Bur-Sin, his son (Third Dynasty, between 2111 and 2113 BCE). They were empty, but their design reflected a change in funeral rites. While the tombs were still situated in an underground vault accessible by a ramp, there were also buildings above ground meant to celebrate the memory of the deceased.

The three-story ziggurat (Etemen Nigur) was built by Ur-Nammu, founder of the Third Dynasty, on the foundations of an older religious edifice. It was then made higher by Nabuchadnezzar II. Monumental staircases recently built give visitors access to the upper level, and a superb view over the site. The façade is scarred by American ordinance from the Gulf War.

Al-Obeid

This site is not known so much for its ruins, but for having given its name to a period of Mesopotamian history (before the flood, between 4300 and 3500 BCE).

The tell, 3.7 miles (6 km) from Ur, was also excavated by Leonard Woolley. It contains the vestiges of a city whose name has not been determined.

Eridu

Eridu, 14 miles (22 km) southwest of Ur, is one of the greatest sacred cities that existed before the deluge. It is said to have been built on the site of an even more ancient village.

The different archaeological strata have enabled researchers to trace human habitation at Eridu from the sixth millennium BCE to the construction of the ziggurat of Ur-Nammu. Third Dynasty kings of Ur built a sanctuary at Eridu to Ea, the God who assembled the earth, and to Marduk's father.

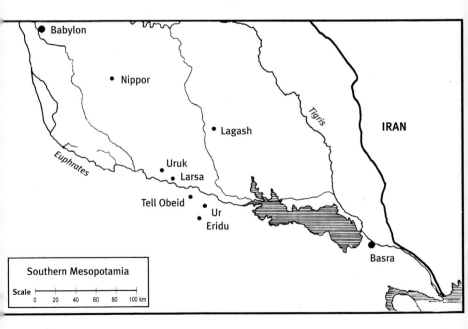

THIRTEEN

From Baghdad to Mosul

Afour-lane highway roughly follows the west bank of the Tigris to Mosul, cutting across its vast meanders. Once out of the suburbs of Baghdad, where the road is usually quite encumbered by farmers' vehicles bringing produce to sell in the markets, the landscape quickly changes as one proceeds northward. Palm trees give way to cultivated fields, crisscrossed with modest irrigation canals. Then comes Samara, which the highway bypasses, and Tikrit. The hills of Jebel Hamrin bring on another, more rugged, landscape. After the Beiji oil refinery, located at the foot of a small mountain range, the road runs between Ashur and Hatra, slaloming between the hills until it reaches Mosul.

Samara, the "Pink City"

In 1912, pottery fragments painted with animal motifs dating from the fifth millennium BCE were discovered in Samara, 84 miles (135 km) northwest of Baghdad. Although its foundation dates from Assyrian times, the city is not mentioned in the chronicles until 836, when Caliph al-Mu'tassim decided to establish his capital there.

King Sennacherib, who called the city Surmarrati, built a fortress there in 690 BCE. We also know that Emperor Julian (Julian the Apostate), mortally wounded at the Battle of Ctesiphon, died at Samara in 363 CE. Convinced that the end of Christianity was near, Julian spoke his last words, "You have vanquished Galilea."

When al-Mu'tassim set his sights on the town in the early 9th century, Baghdad was in a state of deep unrest, with renegade foreign mercenaries threatening the seat of power. The new caliph, who had taken the throne with the help of Turkish soldiers, preferred to move elsewhere rather than face the people's discontent. At the time, Samara was essentially only a Christian monastery surrounded by a cluster of houses.

Al-Mu'tassim was a great architect as well as a great warrior. To build his city he gathered materials and artisans from all over the Islamic world. The result reflected the degree of his ambitions, and earned the admiration of the Caliph's contemporaries. He would call the city *Surraman Ra'a* (Joyful Beholder), but it soon became known as Samara.

The city developed rapidly. The seven caliphs who succeeded each other until 892 each added their own embellishments. Samara had wide avenues, quays and loading docks to accommodate river traffic on the waterfront, twenty palaces built of pink bricks, hunting parks, souks, a viaduct bringing fresh water to the city, three hippodromes, and a zoo. Today, its ruins extend for 19 miles (30 km) along the Tigris.

But the return of the seat of power to Baghdad in 892, and the changing course of the Tigris, were fatal blows to the city. Ravaged by the Mongols, Samara lost most of its inhabitants, and would have ceased entirely to exist were it not for Shi'a pilgrims. A twin mausoleum was built on the site of the house where the Ninth and Tenth Imams (Ali al-Hadi and Hassan al-Askari) were buried, and the Twelfth had "disappeared." The sanctuary has been restored several times. Its current appearance dates from 1869.

Shi'ite influence began to leave its mark on Samara when Mohammad Hassan Shirazi, a religious scholar from Najaf who had proclaimed a *fatwa* against tobacco, started a religious school there in 1875.

The Great Friday Mosque

This mosque was built by al-Mu'tawaqil between 849 and 851. Its impressive dimensions (750 by 500 feet) made it the largest mosque of its time. We know from descriptions that its walls were covered with lacquered porcelain tiles. The edifice is surrounded by 44 towers, in a pattern reminiscent of the Castle of al-Uqaidir, near Karbala. This site somehow escaped destruction at the hands of the Mongols.

The Malwiya

Near the north wall of the Great Mosque stands the Malwiya, a 175-foot tall helicoidal minaret inspired by Mesopotamian ziggurat design. It may have been built before the mosque.

The People's Gate

The Palace of al-Mu'tawaqil (Dar Amir al-Muminin) faced the Tigris. It was almost half a mile long on a side, and was composed of several main buildings, notably Jawsaq al-Khaqani, the residence of the Caliph and his family, excavated by Herzfeld in 1913. He discovered frescoes that disappeared subsequently during transport to Germany during World War I. One of them, reproduced by the archaeologist, portrayed two female dancers. These frescoes decorated the harem.

The three *iwans* that faced the Tigris are all that remains of Dar al-'Ammah, the public section of the palace, where the Caliph held audiences twice a week.

Al-Askariyya Mosque

Relics of Hassan al-Askari (d. 873), who was the Tenth Imam and known as "the Honest One," are buried near the remains of his father, Imam Ali al-Hadi. The cupola of the sanctuary is covered with 72,000 gold plates, and flanked by two minarets.

Next to the mausoleum, the Mosque of the Hidden Imam stands near the entrance to the underground passage where, in 874, the four-year-old Twelfth Imam disappeared (he was called the Mahdi, meaning he who is Guided, or the Master of Time: Shi'ite dogma holds that the Twelfth Imam will return at the end of Time, to restore justice on Earth). The sanctuary is made of two sections that were separated in 1209 by a gate called the Bab al-Ghayba (Gate of the Occultation). On the other side, in one corner of the Room of the Occultation, is the opening of the well from which the Mahdi is supposed to rise.

Environs of Samara

Qasr al-Ashiq

The Castle of the Lover (Qasr al-Ashiq) was built by Caliph al-Mu'tamid shortly before his definitive return to Baghdad at the end of the 9th century. According to certain historians, the caliph was married to a Bedouin girl with whom he was madly in love. His wife pined for her former life as a nomad, so the caliph had a palace built for her in the high country around Samara, where she could see the Tigris floodplain and live as she wished in a Bedouin tent. The castle is about 6 miles (10 km) from Samara. Very well restored, it has a spiral staircase that leads to rooms decorated with clay arabesques.

Mausoleum of Imam al-Douri

The dome of this mausoleum is similar to that of Zubayda's Tomb in Baghdad. Shaykh Mohammad al-Douri is revered by Shi'ites, as a descendant of Imam Mussa al-Kazim (buried in the al-Kazimiyya mosque in Baghdad), and of Ali and Hussein.

The Abu Duluf Mosque

This mosque is a miniature version of the Malwiya. Its minaret is twenty yards high. It stands 14 miles (22 km) from the original, at the end of a long avenue that ran parallel to the river.

Tell al-Sawwan

This Neolithic village 7 miles (11 km) south of Samara was discovered in 1964 along the Tigris, near Samara. Numerous remains date from the 6th millennium BCE, notably statuettes with mother-of-pearl eyes, alabaster figurines of mother goddesses and other objects reminiscent of a phallic cult. The inhabitants of this site seem to have been among the first farmers to use an irrigation system for their crops of wheat and oats.

The tombs that have been unearthed are mostly of children. Their skeletons were wrapped in a thin coating of tar, and enveloped in a casket made of reeds. They were placed with the head facing west, and some had been dismembered. An alabaster phallus was found inside the tombs, no doubt to render the ground more fertile.

Tikrit

Tikrit, one of the most ancient cities of Iraq, is halfway between Baghdad and Mosul. If Saddam Hussein is the city's most famous son today, that honor was held for much longer by the great Arab warrior Saladin (see page 166).

Cuneiform tablets dating from the 9th century BCE attest its existence. In 615 BCE, Nabopolassar failed to seize its citadel, Bitu, built on two hills.

Called "Meonia Tigrides" (Tower of the Tigris) by the Romans and "Tijrit" in Syriac writings, the city was protected for several centuries by an impressive fortress with an octagonal rampart and four main gates.

In 1394, Tikrit was destroyed by Tamerlane and its inhabitants massacred. To punish their resistance and inspire fear in the people, the Mongol emperor had an immense pyramid built with the skulls of the victims. Today, only a few vestiges of the fortress remain, but the reputation for bravery of Tikrit is intact.

Saddam Hussein was born in the village of al-Owja, today a suburb of Tikrit. During his long regime, his house and the school he attended as a child could be visited.

Ahmed Hassan al-Bakr, the first President of the Iraqi Republic after the Revolution of July 1968, was also born in Tikrit. He participated in the overthrow of the monarchy in 1958 by leading an infantry brigade in the occupation of the airbase of Habaniyya. In 1963, he was elected vice president under the regime of Abdel Salam Araf, though he soon resigned his post. He is often referred to as the "Father of the Nation."

Saladin, Victorious against the Crusaders

Salah al-Din al-Ayoubi, known in the West simply as Saladin, was born in Tikrit in 1138. He left the city at an early age for Ba'albeck, where his father, a Kurdish emir and a general in the army of the Sultan of Mosul, had been appointed governor.

At the age of 17, he arrived in Damascus at the court of Sultan Nur al-Din. His uncle, also a general, convinced him to come along on a military expedition to Egypt. For five years, they waged war in the Nile Valley against a local vizier who had concluded an opportunistic alliance with the Crusaders led by Amaury I and headed toward Jerusalem.

Saladin ended up executing the vizier. His uncle was appointed in his place, but died suddenly two months later, in March 1169. The Caliph of Egypt, a Fatimid, opposed to the Baghdadi Abbasids, chose Saladin to replace his uncle, thinking he could easily manipulate him.

But Saladin's political and military acumen quickly revealed itself. He restored order in Egypt. The Franks, concerned with Saladin's rapid rise, landed at Damiette. Defeated, Amaury had to pay a heavy tribute.

Saladin dreamed of liberating Palestine. In 1171, he launched his first expedition, but upon seeing that his forces would be badly outnumbered, he turned back. Back in Egypt, he whittled away the last of the Caliph's powers, and decided to recognize the rival Iraqi sovereign as his own. The Caliph's death soon rendered Saladin master of Egypt.

In May 1174, upon the deaths of Nur al-Din and Amaury I, Saladin became the most powerful man in the Middle East. He was able to devote all his energies to Palestine. He led several battles against the Crusaders. A two-year truce concluded with Beaudoin V was broken by Renaud of Châtillon, who attacked caravans bound for Mecca.

Guy de Lusignan, who succeeded Beaudoin, assembled a force of 20,000 men to fight Saladin. At the Battle of Hattin in 1187, the Crusaders were again defeated, and most of the Frankish lords taken prisoner. Saladin executed Renaud de Châtillon himself. The famous al-Aqsa Mosque was built after he took Jerusalem.

The new Crusade launched by Popes Gregory VIII and Clement III to reconquer the Holy City was immortalized by the troubadours. Saladin and Richard Lionheart became figures of legend. The good King Richard is now cruel (executing 3,000 Muslim prisoners), now the diplomat (considering wedding his sister to Saladin's brother). Several Muslim officers were made knights, but Palestine itself remained Muslim. Crusaders were allowed to enter Jerusalem, but only after leaving their weapons outside the city gates.

Saladin died in February 1193. His memory lives on in the Arab world as a just, pious, wise, and brave prince. He is interred at Damascus, near the Umayyad Mosque; his mausoleum was restored from a dilapidated state by Kaiser Wilhelm II in 1898.

Ashur (Ash-Sharqat)

Founded in the early 3rd millenium BCE, Ashur became the first capital of the Assyrian Empire. It took its name from the national god of the Assyrians (see sidebar on page 168), and would remain its holy city even after the capital moved.

Its site was discovered by Layard in 1847 and excavated by Walter Andrae in 1903–14. Crates filled with finds from the ancient city were sequestered in Lisbon during World War I, and were returned to the Germans only in 1926. Most of these objects are now on display in museums in Berlin and Istanbul.

Ashur is set in a grandiose landscape, atop the rocky escarpment of Jebel Hamrin, which dominates the upper Tigris plain. It is protected to the north by a branch of the Tigris called Umesh Shababit, and to the west and south by a double crenellated wall whose ruins are still standing. A defensive moat followed the wall all around the city, and communicated with the two rivers.

The ziggurat Ashur

The Popular, Bellicose, Pitiless God, Ashur

Ashur was portrayed as a winged man, armed with a bow and arrow, against a radiant sun. He was not only the god of the Assyrian people, but also their military chief. The kings of Ashur declared wars in his name, and called themselves vicars of Ashur. It was he, or his spirit, who led the troops in combat, and it was at his feet that the vanquished gods and pillaged bounty would be laid. All forms of violence were justified in his name, if they served the interests of the Assyrian Empire.

The priests of Ashur had in fact usurped on behalf of their god the attributes of other Mesopotamian divinities, in particular those of Enlil, the supreme being of the Sumerians. They had given Ashur the role of Marduk in the Enuma Elish, the Mesopotamian creation poem. He was the "king of all the gods, the self-created father of the gods."

He resided in the E-Shar-ra with Nin-lil, his principal wife, who was a Sumerian goddess and also the wife of Enlil. Asurbanipal, the last great Assyrian king, was supposedly the "offspring of Ashur and Nin-lil." According to the occasion, the god-king was accompanied in processions by two more wives: Sheroua, "maker of sperm" [sic!] or Ishtar of Erbil, the warrior goddess, sometimes called Ashuritu, simply "the Assyrian."

The god Ashur (National Museum)

The Temple of Ashur (*E-Shar-ra*, the House of Omnipotence) stood on a spit of land where the two rivers joined; it has disappeared, replaced by an Ottoman citadel (the Qishla). Today, it has been restored and is now a museum. The ziggurat of Ashur (*E-hur-sag-gal-kur-kur-ra*, the "Mountain of the Nation"), stands to the left.

This sacred city boasted many other sanctuaries, including the double temples devoted to Sin-Shamash and Anu-Adad, with symmetrical ziggurats.

Upper Tigris Region

Ashur remained a vassal of Ur, Akkad, and finally Babylon until the Assyrian Empire reached its prime, under energetic and cruel kings such as Ashurnazirpal II (883–858 BCE). His rule inaugurated a time of great conquests for the new Assyrian Empire, which would soon extend its borders to the Mediterranean Sea. Vanquished peoples were massively deported to break their resistance. The only other alternative was to pay a massive tribute to the conquerors, which some did.

All the Assyrian kings considered it their sacred duty to embellish the abode of the god Ashur, sometimes by having themselves buried there. German archaeologists have discovered the tombs of three of them; one is that of Ashurnazirpal II; they are confident that they will find many others.

In 140 BCE, Ashur was conquered by the Parthians, who called it Libanae. The restored ruins of the Parthian palace (Qasr al-Awawin, the Palace of Iwans) would be those of a palace built at the time of the kingdom of Hatra. Ashur was sacked by Roman troops in 116 CE, then again overrun by Septimus Severus in 198, and finally destroyed in 257 by Shapur I.

Gorgon head with Aramaic inscription

— FOURTEEN —

Hatra: City of the Sun God

ixty-two miles (100 km) south of Mosul lies Hatra, the most impressive of all of Iraq's great archaeological sites. Although it is officially a UNESCO World Heritage Site, it is ironically one of the country's least known sites. The reason is simple: though it was rediscovered in 1836 by H. J. Ross, a member of the British diplomatic corps in Baghdad, the first description of the city appeared only in 1912. Its author was Walter Andrae, a German archaeologist who was forced to leave Ashur at the outbreak of World War I, when Iraq passed under British dominion.

The four-lane highway that follows the Tigris from Baghdad passes near Hatra on its way to Mosul. In the springtime, as soon as one leaves the palms of Baghdad, the flowers and the greenery are a sharp contrast with the desert landscape to the west, toward Jordan. Past Samara, with its famous helicoidal tower and great 9th-century golden-domed mosque, said to have been the theater of the Twelfth Imam's dramatic disappearance and revered by Shi'a Muslims, one reaches Tikrit, birthplace of Saladin and of Saddam Hussein.

Past the Baiji Refinery, the terrain is full of hills and dales. After the left turn for Ashur, a sign indicates Hatra at 17 miles (28 km) to the left. The country road traverses wheat fields, flowers, and a landscape dotted with small earthen farmhouses. Sheep graze everywhere, and one realizes why this region has long been referred to as Mesopotamia's pantry. The road soon rises progressively, until coming out of a turn, the luminous temples of Hatra mark the horizon.

Hatra (al-Hadhar) is an open-air museum. The city is circular, like the encampments of the nomads who built it, and like Baghdad would be a few centuries later. A mile and a half in diameter, it was protected by a wall that was practically unpassable, doubled by a high ridge, and a moat. While the palaces of the more ancient Mesopotamian cities, built in clay bricks, decomposed relatively rapidly, Hatra has resisted time, for it was built in limestone and marble.

Hatra was a center of commerce and religion. Arab nomads worshipped in Aramaic, the god Shamash (the sun god), Shahiru (the Morning Star, Venus), and Nergal (Mars); an eagle in stone was the sign of these three gods. The temples were all situated in a secure, rectangular area surrounded by its own wall in the center of the city. Inside the sacred perimeter, there are several sanctuaries, one of which is devoted to the Indo-European god, Mithra. Vestiges of colonnades,

The pre-Islamic god Nergal, with his Cerberus (Mosul Museum)

vaults, sculpted reliefs, and *iwans* are all very well preserved. Among the statues of kings and gods, that of Abbu (nicknamed "The Lady of Hatra") is perhaps the most remarkable. The city is an incredible mix of architectural styles, with Parthian, Greek, Roman, and Persian influences – all peoples with whom the local bedouins had to contend.

An Incredible Synthesis of Cultures

From Hatra's outer walls (an earthen ridge or berm, reinforced by mud bricks, built to retard an enemy assault), the stone walls of the city proper are visible, about 1,500 feet away. They are huge, and ring the city completely, with regularly spaced towers and gates. The well-preserved northern gate gives a good idea of the security measures taken to protect the city. One has to cross the moat, and pass through two gates separated by a courtyard from which defenders could watch and fire upon entrants through narrow holes in the courtyard walls. To the left, the small building that once housed the statue of Hercules (before the recent war on display in Baghdad) is intact.

In the heart of the city, still three-quarters buried, stands the *temenos* with its sanctuaries, a rectangular esplanade surrounded by a wall of cut blocks of stone along which the merchants of the time had their boutiques. Facing the main east entrance, on the other side of the vast expanse, is the Temple of Shamash. On either side stand statues of other divinities such as Shahiru, whose spells stopped evildoers, and Nergal, with his three-headed dog. The restoration of the temple is indistinguishable from the original vestiges, and the honey-colored stone shines warmly in a deep blue sky. Few places in the world are capable of provoking the intensity of emotion one feels at dawn in Hatra. When the first rays of the sun hit the *iwans* and sanctuaries, their domed rooms seem to open up to the east, and breathe life into the sculpted eagles on the walls, and the altars themselves.

Among the statues of kings and gods that have been recovered are those of Hatran noblemen and warlords, dressed in rich robes, some with Phrygian bonnets. The most beautiful is that of Abbu, the "Lady of Hatra," once on display in Baghdad. A copy stands in the courtyard opposite the temples, but has been damaged by vandals.

A Hellenistic temple in Hatra

A team of Italian archaeologists was digging at Hatra during our visit. Roberta Ricciardi, head of the team, is a professor at the University of Turin, who fell in love with Hatra and goes there every year in the spring, practically at her own expense; government funding of archaeological expeditions in Iraq all but dried up after the 1991 Gulf War.

Arab Kings

Our tour guide, Ismail Rashid Ali, once a restorer of antiques could talk enthusiastically about Hatra for hours. In his view, as long as the royal palace and especially the library have not been found, it is difficult to reconstitute the history of the city. The inscriptions in Aramaic at the bottom of walls or statues enable us to date the buildings and often the sovereign who had ordered their construction. Arab authors of the first centuries CE affirm that Hatra was built on the site of a more ancient Assyrian fortress. Peasants took refuge on the plateau after the fall of Nineveh in 612 BCE and built a village there. Later on, the inhabitants added sanctuaries devoted to the gods of the time, to attract bedouins and increase trade with the surrounding area. As a stopover for caravans travelling between Ctesiphon and Anatolia, Hatra developed rapidly.

Hatra is said to have been founded at this site of an ancient Assyrian fortress (which dates from the mid-3rd century BCE) in the second century BCE with the aid of the Parthians, a warrior tribe from the Caspian region. The Parthians had created an empire on the remains of that of Alexander the Great. Hatra's position at the outskirts of this Empire, between the Tigris and the Euphrates (river routes that all invaders of Mesopotamia had followed), gave the city a strategic role. At its beginnings, the city was governed by a group of Arab shaykhs and priests. Then, a dynasty of kings took over, allied to the Parthians, but independent to a large degree. From 156 to 241, its kings, including Nasser, Lajash, Sanatruq I, Abd Samia, and Sanatruq III, held the title "Emir of the Arabs." The emirs of Hatra paid a tribute to the Parthians, who considered the city an outpost against the Romans, who were occupying Syria and vying to gain control of the Silk Road.

The Fall of Hatra

Twice, Hatra resisted the assaults of Romans intent on gaining control of the Silk Road. In 117, Emperor Trajan abandoned a siege of the city; the historian Dion Cassius says that he found the region too inhospitable for settlement. In 193, Septimus Severus launched a campaign against Abd Samia I (Barsemius for the Romans) to punish him for having supported Pescennius Niger, one of Septimus' rivals, in his bid for power in Rome. The siege lasted six months. A breach opened in the wall by the Romans was filled during the night by the inhabitants of the city; when the Roman troops finally mutinied, the siege was lifted in haste. The heat was atrocious, and many were sick, not to mention tired of the Hatrans' cunning and innovative defensive tactics. In addition to the famous "Fires of Hatra" (arrows with flaming tips), there were also projectiles containing scorpions and wasps.

Things played out differently in 241. After the fall of the Parthian empire, Hatra had become a Roman ally. The Persians, new masters of the region, were resolved to stamp out this pocket of resistance. Historians are undecided as to who defeated the Hatrans, hesitating between Ardashir, founder of the Sassanid dynasty, and Shapur I. Arab historians tend to prefer the latter, favoring the story of Nadira's betrayal.

Nadira was the daughter of al-Dhaizen, the last king of Hatra, a Persian. She was in love with Shapur, her great uncle and enemy of Hatra. In exchange for a marriage promise, she revealed the secret of the Talisman that protected the walls of the city, giving away the password. She did marry Shapur, but after a while, the Persian king decided that she would betray him too. After a quarrel, he had her attached to a horse and dragged on the ground in the plain of Karbala until she died.

In fact, according to a document discovered during excavations in Egypt, the city surrendered to escape famine and epidemics. It took a year-long siege for Shapur to take the city in 250, which was then pillaged and definitively abandoned ten years later.

One may wonder why the Romans, who had a garrison at Hatra, did not send reinforcements. Amianus Marcellinus, who passed near the city with the Roman legions in 364, could only assess the ruins.

Thieves of the Past

In the run-up, and then the aftermath, of the spring 2003 bombing of Iraq, art historians and archeologists around the world were desperate to do something to protect the more than 10,000 known archeological sites and invaluable museum collections that hold Iraq's great cultural legacy. The last decade, since the 1991 Gulf War, had been a dismal one for anyone concerned with the state of antiquities and the preservation of heritage in Iraq, and many hoped to avoid the destruction caused by the earlier Gulf War.

Precautions taken at the end of 1990, before the bombing began in January, were not sufficient. At the time, Moayed Said, then director of Iraq's Board of Antiquities, had the National Museum's collections placed in a secure location, but he had not predicted the scale of destruction that would ensue in the Gulf War, or the thefts that would plague the country afterwards.

During the 1991 conflict, over 4,000 pieces disappeared from different museums. The Basra Museum was sacked; the museum in Mosul escaped the same fate with the protection of the Iraqi Army. American bombs damaged or destroyed ancient mosques and churches, and cracked or collapsed dozens of other structures, such as the great arch of the Palace of Ctesiphon. The ziggurat of Ur is riddled with shrapnel scars. According to an Italian scholar, American soldiers blew tank shells into the ancient tells. After a complaint was lodged at the UN by the Iraqi Minister of Cultural Affairs, a crate of stolen objects was returned to Iraq by the United States.

A list of 2,000 pieces was made public in 1992, and sent to the world's foremost museums and auction houses. Some of these pieces have reappeared on the art market, in the United States, Europe, and Japan. The British government seized two important pieces that were on sale at Christie's in London. Said points out that if "the demand in other countries was not so high, there wouldn't be so many thefts."

Faced with the gargantuan task of protecting thousands of sites and 33 museums, Said took draconian measures. But he couldn't put a guard in front of each of Iraq's temples. Toward the end of the 1990s, the museums of Baghdad and Mosul were still mostly closed, except for the lucky few with a written permit from the Board of Antiquities. In the rooms behind locked doors, only the large pieces, too difficult to move, remained; many display cases were empty.

In early 1998, an Iraqi newspaper announced that looters were going to be executed for having sliced up one of the winged bulls' heads taken from the temple of Sargon II (721–705 BCE) at Khorsabad, the fourth Assyrian capital. In the end, their sentence was commuted to a prison term. The pieces of the head, found by the Iraqi police, were taken to the National Museum in Baghdad. An Army guard was placed at the site.

The statue at Khorsabad weighed thirty tons, was 10 feet long and almost 7 feet high. But the thieves had professional tools: scaffolding, a generator, and a powerful electric saw. Usually, thieves are more poorly equipped and work with the fearful haste of amateurs. At Nimrud, thieves broke in two a marble plaque bearing an engraving of the Assyrian Tree of Life.

But international art traffickers are not lacking in imagination. Iraqi police have even confiscated copies of statuettes and jewels meant to replace the originals in museums. Of course poverty pushes some individuals to commit these acts: with the long years of embargo, and now war again, it must be tempting to look for riches under the ground. In Iraq, it suffices to know where to dig to find something. In the 1950s, a favorite weekend pastime for foreign

Winged bull's head sawn up by looters

diplomats was "telling." A little black book secretly detailed all the interesting places to look for artifacts. After a picnic and siesta, all you had to do was dig for a few minutes, and out came a piece of pottery or another interesting, if not valuable, object.

But the fact remains: every broken tablet, every missing artifact, is not just an Iraqi loss, but a loss for all humanity.

For an assessment of post-war damage to the major sites and cultural institutions of Iraq, go to www.nationalgeographic.com. In May 2003, *National Geographic* sent teams of experts and photographers to northern and southern Iraq to investigate the damage.

A few Arab poets lamented the disaster, and Hatra became a field of ruins where bedouins grazed their sheep and worshipped their gods, until the Islamization of Iraq. Broken heads of statues found at Hatra are the work of the first Muslim idol-breakers.

The beautiful Arab calligraphy carved on the wall of the south *iwan* dates from Ottoman times. In the 13th century, the Turkish governors of Mosul, known for their love of the arts and architecture, started restoring buildings and using them as barracks.

A Site in Danger

As our tour guide often reminded us, Hatra still holds mysteries. After walking through the dim light of a long, vaulted, partially restored corridor, the temple of Shamash appears. Here, Arabs from all over the Middle East once gathered to worship as they do in Mecca today, for Hatra is the oldest of the sacred cities of Islam. But that is not all. Another Arab temple, built in the year 85, holds even more mystery. It is dedicated to a "Supreme Triad" that is still a subject of debate among archaeologists and historians: Maran, "Our Lord" (sometimes represented by an eagle with folded wings, also the symbol of Hatra), his wife Martan "Our Lady," and their son Bar Marin, "Son of our Two Lords." Scholars have not yet been able to piece together the historical and religious significance of this pre-Islamic holy family, which bears a striking resemblance to the Christian Trinity. It has been said that the Magi who visited Christ passed through Hatra.

One cannot leave Hatra without sharing the concerns of Ricciardi, the Italian archaeologist, about the future of these important traces of the Arabs' past, given the damage suffered during a decade of embargo, the war, and the uncertain times ahead. Most of the statues have been protected from theft by brick enclosures or simply by walling off sections of the temples. But Sharif, the lone guard who walked a beat around the site armed with an old Russian Simonov rifle, might not scare off all the "head-hunters" that prowl the environs. And looting became widespread after the US invasion of 2003. As for erosion and weathering, which has caused walls to collapse and columns to crumble, nothing can scare that off, except a concerted international effort to preserve the site. Ricciardi would like to create an association, the "Friends of Hatra" to make the general public more aware of the fate that awaits Hatra if nothing is done soon.

Until now, the multiple appeals to work toward the preservations of Iraqi archaeological sites have fallen on deaf ears, in spite of the principles put forth in the Hague Convention on the Protection of Cultural Treasures.

The Nuri minaret

FIFTEEN

Mosul and Environs

Mosul is situated on the west bank of the Tigris, near Nineveh, 250 miles (400 km) from Baghdad. First called Khawlan, then Budh Ardashir, after the first Sassanid sovereign, Mosul's foundation harkens back to a mythical past.

Christianity has been present in the area since the second century. A convent built in the 5th century, then turned into a fortress, was the epicenter of the city's subsequent development. Under Caliph Omar, the Christian citadel was taken by the Arab troops of Utba Ibn Farkad in 641. Mosul became, under Umayyad rule, the capital of the province of Jezireh. Its influence would wane with that of the Abbasid caliphate.

Under the Seljuk Turks, the *attabeqs*, or governors, of Mosul were quite powerful. One of them, Imad al-Din Zengi, was practically an independent ruler, who brought Mosul back to something of its former splendor.

In the 13th century, Prince Badr al-Din Lulu became an ally of the Mongol leader, Hulagu, to save Mosul from destruction. But the city was plundered nevertheless in 1259, to punish the prince's son who had not respected the terms of the agreement. Some years later, Tamerlane had the tombs of Jonas (Nabi Younes) and Girgis (Saint George) restored.

After the Ottomans took Mosul in 1637, its fortunes declined. It was devastated by a terrible earthquake in 1667. Besieged for six months by the Persians under Nadir Shah, the city resisted triumphantly. The Turks ended up granting certain liberties to the Mosulite family of Abdel Jalily, and administrative privileges over the city.

The *vilayat* (province) of Mosul became part of the French zone of influence under the Sykes-Picot Agreement concluded between Britain

Ruins of Bash Tapia, a 12th-century fortress

and France during World War I; in May 1919, the French government accepted its cession to the new Iraqi monarchy.

Mosul has a souk and numerous historical monuments, notably mosques and old churches. The city gave its name to the word "mousseline," a light muslin made of cotton and sometimes silk.

The remains of the palace of Badr al-Din Lulu, built in the 13th century, called Qara Serai (the Black Palace), stand on the west bank of the Tigris. Only the ends of two large rooms and their arched vaults are still standing. Sculpted figures dating from the Islamic period are a rarity, however, for human representation was forbidden in Islam.

On the banks of the Tigris, a stretch of wall of Bash Tipia (a 12th-century fortress built by the Ottomans) is still standing. The *attabegs* had transformed the place into a munitions depot. Most of the fortifications were destroyed in 1915, then razed in 1934. From the summit, one can see all of Mosul and Nineveh in the distance.

The Mosul Museum

The Mosul Museum was inaugurated on the occasion of the millennial anniversary of the birth of Avicenna (980–1037), the philosopher and doctor whose influence on Arab thought was so profound. It is the biggest museum in Iraq after Baghdad's. Because of the archaeological wealth of the region (which contains the sites of Nimrud, Nineveh, Khorsabad, and Hatra, among others), its collections of monumental art and precious objects are the envy of museums worldwide. Among the statues of gods, the most interesting for students of history are those of Maran, Martan, and Bar Marin.

In another room, tools and pottery of great beauty are on display; they were discovered in the tumulus of Hassuna, 22 miles (35 km) south of Mosul, or at Halaf on the Turko-Syrian river (the Khabur), or at Neolithic sites such as Tell Affar and Nemrik.

During the 1991 Gulf War, the Iraqi Army guarded the museum, saving its treasures from looting. American bombs did not spare Hatra or Nimrud, where several statues were damaged. At Mosul, churches were hit by missiles, and the Hadba minaret was cracked. At Nineveh, part of St. Thomas' Church was damaged by shrapnel. In the 2003 war, the museum was not directly hit by cruise missiles, but according to a National Geographic research team, the mueum's large plate-glass windows were damaged. Thieves had stolen parts of bronze reliefs from the Balawat gates in the Assyrian gallery, as well as some smaller items.

Mosques and Islamic Sanctuaries

• The minaret of the mosque of the Umayyads is the oldest Muslim religious edifice in the city. It dates from the taking of the city by Utba Ibn Farkad.

• The Nuri minaret is known for its strong resemblance to the Leaning Tower of Pisa. It is said to have listed this way upon the death of the Prophet Mohammad, to salute his rise to Paradise. It was part of the great mosque built by the *attabeg* Zengi in 1172.

• The Prophet Girgis (Saint George) is said to be interred in the mosque that bears his name, which was first renovated in 1393. This mosque was visited by the great Arab voyager, Ibn Batuta.

• The Mujahidi Mosque (12th century) boasts a beautiful dome and wrought *mirhab*. It is also known as the al-Qidr, or Red Mosque.
• The sanctuary of the Imam Yahyla Abdul Qassem, on the west bank of the Tigris, dates from the 13th century. It was built by Bar-Eddine Lulu and is situated near the Bash Tapia fortress. It is easily recognizable by its conical dome. It is graced by beautiful calligraphies engraved in blue marble.

Jonas's Tomb

The Muslim sanctuary of Nabi Younes (the Prophet Jonas, who lived in the early 7th century BCE), recently restored, was actually a Nestorian church built on the ruins of a "fire-temple" or Mazdean sanctuary. This had been in turn built on top of an Assyrian edifice.

In the Qur'an, Jonas is known as the "Man of the Fish." Mohammad had a special affection for Jonas, and even said, as a famous *hadith* reports, "that nobody should ever hold Mohammad above Younes." The great fish that swallowed Jonas at Nineveh is said to have cast him up onto a red stone, which was later known for its curative powers. It has now disappeared.

Jonas's tomb

Recent digs underneath the foundations of Jonas' tomb have unearthed huge stone heads of winged bulls. It is surmised that this was the site of the palace of Asarhadon (681–669 BCE), the son of Asurbanipal. In 1954, Iraqi archaeologists found nearby statues brought back from Egypt by this Assyrian prince.

The memory of Jonas is very much alive in the region of Mosul. A mosque and several *khans* or caravanserais were built in the 10th century at Tell al-Tawba, at the place where Nabi Younes was endeavoring to convert the local people to monotheism.

Churches

The old churches of Mosul are mostly of Nestorian origin. Their aspect is quite austere. The following are worth visiting:

• Mar Thomas, built in 770. Inscriptions in Garsuni (Arabic written in Syriac characters, or Aramean) indicate that it was restored in 1744. A niche contains relics of St. Thomas, who was known for having preached in India.

• Tahra of the Chaldeans, situated near the Bash Tapia fortress, was founded in the mid-7th century, and restored in 1743. Devoted to the Virgin Mary, it is said to have been built on the ruins of a more ancient church. Worshippers can pray before an 18th-century marble icon.

• Sim'un al-Safa, built between the 4th and 7th centuries, and restored in the 14th century. This church boasts numerous inscriptions in Syriac.

• Mar Hudeni, named after a Christian martyr from Tikrit who died in 575, was founded in the 10th century. Above the door, one can see a beautiful 13th-century lintel. People come from afar to drink the mineral water from a source that runs in the courtyard, and pray wrapped in a chain attached to a wall, which is famed for its ability to calm epileptics.

Monasteries and Convents Around Mosul

Qaraqosh

The name of this village 19 miles (30 km) southeast of Mosul means "black bird" in Turkish. Christians called it Bagdede (House of God), a

Persian name that appeared during the Sassanid epoch.

The people of Qaraqosh are said to have converted to Christianity in the 6th century. Like other villages in the region, it was ravaged by the Mongols and plundered by the Persians under Nadir Shah in 1743. Numerous Christian families, originally from Tikrit, emigrated there during the 11th and 12th centuries.

With only 20,000 inhabitants, there are ten Christian churches. They are mostly Chaldean or Jacobite. The biggest is al-Tahira, "the Immaculate," inaugurated in 1948. Built by the village's inhabitants out of Mosul's yellow marble, it is obviously less interesting in design than the original al-Tahira, which still stands next to the new church. Its foundations date from 1219. In the nave reserved for women, there is an ancient baptismal font, covered with liturgical inscriptions.

One should not leave Qaraqosh without seeing Bne Smuni, a small Jacobite church situated in the southern section of the village. On the lintel of an intricately worked door, one can admire a female figure seated between two lions.

Mar Benham, Convent of the Cistern

This convent is situated 22 miles (35 km) east of Mosul, near Nimrud, capital of the Assyrian Empire and Qaraqosh.

According to legend, Saint Behnam was the son of King Sennacherib, and converted to Christianity after meeting a hermit who miraculously healed his sister of leprosy. Sennacherib did not appreciate his son's conversion: he had his two children executed, and buried underneath a cistern. A mausoleum, then a fortified church, were subsequently built nearby. Nearby is a small pond, known for what the local inhabitants say has a natural ability to heal certain skin diseases.

In spite of the anachronism (Mar Behnam was a Christian martyr, but he lived during Sassanid times, between the 3rd and 6th centuries), the legend is still widely believed.

The convent served for a long time as a hostel for pilgrims en route to Jerusalem. After it was pillaged in 1295, a monk named Yacoub decided to "convert" Saint Behnam to Islam in order to protect the place from further depredations. He even supplied him with a new identity,

Surely, this place is a holy place, where a saint of miraculous powers rests. Whoever invokes him will be blessed with good fortune. Carry yourselves with respect and compunction, and prostrate yourselves before the Holy Cross, and pray to our Saint so that the Lord will have mercy on us, and will not forsake us, thanks to his intercession.

—Aramaic inscription engraved on the walls of the Mar Behnam sanctuary

Mar Behnam convent

as a sort of double of Qidr, a mythical character in the Qur'an. The convent subsequently became a place of pilgrimage for Muslims and Yezidis, and its sculptures were saved.

The church of Mar Behnam is considered one of the most beautiful oriental churches of the 12th and 13th centuries. The doors are decorated with a lion's head (emblem of the Turkish *attabegs* of Mosul) and the frames wrought with intricate friezes made of inscriptions in Syriac capital letters. On the frame of the northern-facing outer door, there are friezes representing Saint Peter and Saint Paul, Saint Behnam

Bust of Maran, "Our Lord," also known as Shamash, the sun god (Mosul Museum)

and Saint Sarah, on either side of a cross. A niche in pink marble is built into the outer façade of the church, surrounded by smaller lateral niches and intricate friezes.

Inside the church, one of the doors is decorated with 21 escutcheons whose frames are made of carved intertwined serpents. Each escutcheon contains a cross, each of which is carved in a different design. The friezes of the royal door of the sanctuary date from 1164. On its lintel, on either side, Saint Behnam and Saint George are depicted slaying a dragon. Saint Behnam's tomb is on one side of the cistern, in a niche framed by sculpted flowers. Not far from the sanctuary is the entrance to an underground passage, which led to Nimrud.

On Saint Behnam's Day, Christians of the region prepare the dish that he ate for his last supper: a mix of raisins, chickpeas, fava beans, and wheat.

The convent's library possesses beautiful old Syriac and Arab manuscripts.

Saint Michael's Monastery

Built in the 4th century by a monk named Michael, this monastery is situated on the west bank of the Tigris, 4 miles (6 km) north of Mosul. At the time, as many as 300 monks lived there. The library used to have many rare manuscripts, which are now dispersed in Western museums.

The monastery was rebuilt several times without fundamental modifications to the original design, notably in the 13th century under the reign of Badr-Eddin Lulu, attabeg of Mosul. The church is the oldest building. It has three beautiful marble arches.

A tomb said to be that of Saint Michael is visible on the south side of the church.

Archaeological digs conducted in the environs have uncovered the ruins of two more monasteries.

Mar Girgis (Saint George) Convent

Saint George's Convent is situated on a tell about 6 miles (10 km) from Mosul, on the road to Dohuk. The church that is attached to the convent was originally that of the village of Ba'wira, which moved further south as the course of the Tigris changed. In the church, which was restored in 1843, a painting portrays St. George on horseback, slaying a dragon. The scene is drawn from an old Sumerian legend.

Saint George was a Roman officer from Palestine. He was executed in 303, for having symbolically torn up in public a decree by the Emperor Dioclitian. He intended by his sacrifice to encourage other Christians to stand up for their faith, at a time when their resolve was being taxed by Roman persecution.

The Mar Matti (Saint Matthew) Monastery

Looking more like a fortress, the Mar Matti Monastery dominates the plain from the flanks of the Mount Maqloub, 22 miles (35 km) northwest of Mosul.

It was established in the 4th century by Saint Matthew (Mar Matti), a Syriac monk originally from Diyarbakir, in Turkish Kurdistan. He had fled the persecution of Julian the Apostate. Thousands of monks came to join him there. Jebel al-Faf, where it is located, has come to be known among Christians as the Mount of Thousands.

Its rich library lost precious manuscripts when Persians looted it in the 4th century, and again in the 13th century to the Mongols.

Al-Qosh

According to legend, this village 28 miles (45 km) from Mosul was founded by a Jew named Alqone, who had been deported by the

Assyrians. But Al-Qosh is mostly known for being one of the oldest Christian villages in northern Iraq, and the birthplace of the Old Testament Prophet Nahum.

Al-Qosh's history, partly tied to that of the monastery of Rabban Hormiz, can only be described as tragic. The village was destroyed by the White Sheep Turkomans (see Chapter 2) in 1508, then plundered by the Persians under Nadir Shah in 1743, whose troops hunted down the inhabitants in the mountains, and, according to chronicles, "made them suffer outrages that cannot be described or recounted." It was sacked by the Kurdish princes of Rowandruz in 1832, then again in 1842 by the Kurdish princes of Amadya. Famine struck Al-Qosh in 1879. It is said that the twelve priests of al-Qosh were not sufficient to administer the last rites to all the dying.

The Mar Georgis Church here is quite old. In 1906, when it was last restored, stones from a sculpted cross were found, bearing traces of blood that could be as old as St. George himself. They have been sealed in the walls of the edifice, to the right of the main altar.

Ownership of the tomb of Nahum the Prophet (three-quarters of which is situated underground) was long disputed between Christians and Jews. One day, a Jew, furious at not being granted rights over the tomb, desecrated it by replacing the bones with those of a sheep or donkey. The relics of Prophet Nahum were allegedly hidden in the church of Mar Miha, and are supposedly still there. A plaque indicates that the relics are housed to the left of the altar door.

Rabban Hormiz Monastery

This monastery is carved in rock, and dominates the valley of al-Qosh, a mile and a half from Our Lady of Harvests. The approach is rather rugged, up a rocky path and stone steps.

The monastery is temporarily uninhabited, for the area is not secure at night. Tension and instability reigning in this region near the border of Kurdistan have made the area a favorite hangout for smugglers.

The brave can visit the smoke-blackened rooms that tunnel into the mountain. In a crypt dug under the church, monks used to conduct exorcisms. Christians supposedly possessed by demons were locked up for a night there, in chains attached to the stone wall.

In 630, one of the cells was occupied by Rabban Hormiz, the monk who gave his name to the monastery. The rings from which he had himself hung by the hands to be flagellated are still fixed in the ceiling.

Archaeological Sites Around Mosul

Nineveh

The main entrance to Nineveh (Ninawa in Assyrian) is located right outside Mosul, on the Kosser River that crosses the city. When a National Geographic team of archeologists went into Iraq to investigate damage to sites in May 2003, after the second Gulf War, they found that new suburbs had encroached upon the ancient site, and that a general decay had taken place over the 13 years of war and sanctions.

Nineveh is thought to have been founded by Ninus, who later married the beautiful Samiramis. This king, according to Ctesias (a Greek doctor of the 6th–5th centuries BCE), wanted to build "a city which should be many times bigger than any other city, so that even in the future, a larger city would not exist." Ninus called it Nineveh, which simply means "the abode of Ninus." Manishtusu (2235–2321 BCE), son of Sargon of Akkad, added a temple to the goddess Ishtar. A thousand years later, Tigrit-Pelisar I (1117–1077 BCE) built a royal residence. Nineveh finally became the third capital of the Assyrian Empire (after Ashur and Nimrud) under the reign of Sennacherib (705–681 BCE). His father, Sargon II, was about to transfer the capital to Khorsabad when he was assassinated. According to Herodotus, the city had a population of around 300,000.

The tell of Kuyunjik (the "little sheep") was initially excavated in 1842 by Paul-Emile Botta (1802–1870), the French Consul at Mosul. But the archaeologist soon left this site to dig in the ruins of Khorsabad, which seemed to hold greater promise. Sir Henry Layard resumed research at the site of Sennacherib's palace, discovering a fresco showing the king seated on his throne, receiving plunder from the city of Lakish—an episode mentioned in the Old Testament (Kings). By the end of his tenure at Nineveh, Taylor had unearthed ten winged bulls, two thousand reliefs, and part of Asurbanipal's library (668–626 BCE). It housed one of the most important collections of literary, scientific and religious works of ancient times, totaling several thousand tablets.

After Layard left, his assistant, a Chaldean named Hormuzd Rassam (1826–1910), led nocturnal excavations of a section of the site allocated to France, violating an agreement concluded with Victor Place. In 1854, he discovered the famous injured lioness, as well as the rest of Asurbanipal's library. But these digs were carried out haphazardly, without taking the necessary precautions, and ended up ruining the vestiges of buildings razed in 612 (when a coalition of Scythians, Medes, and Babylonians—led by Nabuchadnezzar, then still a prince—attacked the city).

Serious digs resumed in 1927. Max Malloyan unearthed a stone head representing Sargon of Akkad, and did a stratigraphic study, going almost 30 yards underground. Habitation of the site was dated back to 6000 BCE.

The wall of Nineveh, eight miles long (12 km), has been partially restored, as have been the gates of Maska and Shamash. The Gate of Nergal now houses the museum of Nineveh, which looters had tried

Monastery of al-Qosh

unsuccessfully to break into in the wake of the American bombing in the spring of 2003. Presumably, the models of the main Assyrian cities are still on display.

Near Ain Sifni, 32 miles (52 km) north of Mosul, a monumental fresco carved in the rock several yards above ground level shows Sennacherib kneeling before Ashur and Ninlil. This marks the entrance to the oldest canal in the world, one that brought fresh water to Nineveh. Lined in stone, it wound its way more than fifty miles (80 km) to Nineveh.

Khorsabad (Dur Shuruqin)

This city 12 miles (20 km) northeast of Mosul was discovered in 1843 by Paul-Emile Botta, with the help of a villager. Digs unearthed many reliefs with hunting and war scenes and huge winged bulls. But work was soon interrupted by the Turkish governor of the *vilayat* of Mosul, who thought that the archeologists' camp, with its trenches, was the outpost of an invading army! (In 2003, the trenches dug in various parts of the site were in fact those of an army: in this case, the the Iraqi army itself. They do not seem to have harmed artifacts.)

When the 19th-century digs resumed with the arrival of the great draftsman Eugène Flandin and the necessary official clearances in Constantinople. On May 1, 1847, the Assyrian gallery of the Louvre was inaugurated in grand ceremony, with the best of the treasure unearthed at the site.

After the departure of Botta, Victor Place (1818–1875) quickly got to work. Layard had taken advantage of the interruption to do exploratory drilling, and he had found a number of winged genies and bulls with human heads. The French archaeologist unearthed the palace of Sargon (Dur Shuruqin), a set of buildings that included a temple, a seven-story ziggurat (probably surrounded by a continuous ramp), and more than 200 pieces, over an area of ten hectares. Hundreds of frescoes, statues, weapons, and various other objects were recovered.

Sargon II (721–705 BCE) had brought the kingdoms of Israel and Judea under his control, and taken Cyprus and Babylon. He wanted to magnify his reign by building a new capital, as his great predecessors had done. He had chosen the village of Haganuda, north of Nineveh, as the site for the most beautiful palace ever built in Assyria. Work on the palace began in 713 BCE and ended in 707. But Sargon II died only two years after moving into his new residence.

The discoveries of Victor Place considerably enriched the already fabulous collections of the Louvre, even if he didn't manage to get it all back to Paris. The precious cargo was transported down the Tigris on *keleks* (rafts placed on floaters made of inflated animal skins), but ran aground near Kurna. Only part of the treasure was saved. The rest, including several winged bulls, sleeps under tons of river mud (see Chapter 10), where it is at least safe from looters, and probably even the unexploded bombs that pepper this site and many others throughout Iraq.

Agatha Christie Discovers Nimrud

"On one of our days off, we decided to rent a car to go and have a look at the great hill of Nimrud, which had been excavated by Layard a hundred years before. It wasn't easy going for Max, driving across the countryside streaked with wadis and irrigation canals often impossible to cross. But in the end, we arrived and had our luncheon in a spectacular setting. The Tigris flowed a short distance away, and out of the top of the huge mound covering the acropolis, massive stones reared their heads. You could even see the gigantic wing of a stone genie. It was a powerful sight, full of the mystery and romanticism of a long-gone past."

—Agatha Christie,
An *Autobiography*

Nimrud (Kalakh)

Situated on the Tigris south of Mosul, about 6 miles (10 km) upstream of the junction with the Great Zab River, and 23 miles (37 km) southeast of Mosul, the city of Kalakh (Kellek in the Old Testament) was the Assyrians' military capital. It was founded by Salmanazar I (1274–1245 BCE) and populated in large part by deported Babylonians. It was to enter a period of expansion under Asurnazirpal II (884-958 BCE), who made it his capital. Thanks to the accumulated treasure of his conquests and thousands of slaves, he built a city that would defy time.

The citadel-palace is surrounded by a wall almost 100 feet thick. This fortified defensive wall runs almost five miles (8 km) , and is flanked by numerous towers. The Tigris, which is today about a mile and a half away, used to run along the fortifications. For the inauguration, Asurnazirpal organized a sumptuous ten-day banquet, reportedly attended by 169,574 guests.

Sir Henry Layard thoroughly plundered the site for ten years, to the great benefit of the British Museum. With his acolyte, the unscrupulous Hormuzd Rassam, brother of a British vice consul in Mosul, he set out on a frenetic hunt for frescoes and statues. Reliefs were literally hacked out of the walls, with no regard for the surrounding structures. The best pieces were shipped to London, leaving the remainder exposed to the elements.

The hill of Nimrud yielded an unexpected wealth of treasure. The palace of Asurnazirpal II was decorated with numerous winged, human-headed bulls and lions, and sculpted, engraved reliefs adorning the walls. It was literally plundered. In the palace of Salmanazar III (858–824 BCE), restored by Tigrat Pelisar (745–727 BCE), looters discovered Salmanazar's famous "black obelisk," which depicts the scene of the tribute of Jehu, king of Israel, as it was reported in the Old Testament. By the end of his work, Layard had removed no less than thirteen couples of winged bulls and lions, reliefs recounting the victories of kings, dozens of alabaster vases, bronze statues and weaponry, ivory sculpture, and a throne in ornamental wood decorated with bronze plaques. It is perhaps the largest single theft of the Iraqi cultural heritage ever committed (see Chapter 14 sidebar, for more on art theft).

Fortunately, research was continued in a more scientific manner by Max Mallowan (1949–1963). Assisted by a team of professionals, including his wife, Agatha Christie, he uncovered palaces, temples and, at the bottom of a well, a woman's head in ivory. Agatha Christie washed off the millennia of mud, and baptized it the "Mona Lisa of Nimrud." Mallowan tried to limit the damage caused by Layard, but it was too late to undo it.

A team of Iraqi archaeologists took over the site in 1970. They reconstituted the palace of Asurnazirpal II with its winged bulls and reliefs. The tombs of queens and princesses from the 8th–7th centuries BCE were discovered, with over 400 pieces of jewelry, in a royal vault whose walls were decorated with precious stones.

"Great Hunter before the Eternal"

The Old Testament gives the following genealogy: Cush, the son of Shem (whose father, Noah, was saved from the Deluge with his three sons, and recreated the human race), fathered Nimrud.

"And Cush begat Nimrud: he began to be a mighty one in the earth. He was a mighty hunter before the Lord: wherefore it is said, Even as Nimrud the mighty hunter before the Lord. And the beginning of his kingdom was Babel, and Erech, and Akkad, and Calneh, in the land of Shinar. Out of that land went forth Asshur, and built the city of Nineveh, and the city Rehoboth, and Calah, And Resen between Nineveh and Calah: the same is a great city."
—Genesis 10

Nimrud was destroyed at the same time as Nineveh by the Babylonian coalition of 612, and abandoned. Alexander the Great camped with his army at the foot of the ziggurat's ruins, before facing the Persian, Darius III, in the plain of Gaugameles.

Today, these ruins still stand some 50 feet high. Some historians say that the ziggurat used to have a spiral ramp providing access to the summit, similar to the Malwiya at Samara. Besides the palace of Asurnazirpal, one can visit the temple of Nabu, which has been very well restored. The huge field of ruins still holds many secrets. In the summer of 2003, it was US soldiers who stood guard over them, 24 hours a day.

Two and a half miles (4 km) from Nimrud, one can see the village of Selamiya, on the site of an ancient city, Resen, an Assyrian city mentioned in the Old Testament.

Village of Bahzani, with Yezidi sanctuaries

The Yezidis

The Yezidis are a very ancient but little-known religious community, though they have been around since well before the start of Islam, before even the beginnings of Christianity, and maybe since the time when the first Indo-European religions began.

For Muslims, the Yezidis were partisans of the Umayyad Caliph Yazid (680–683), who took refuge in Kurdistan during the Abbasid epoch. For Muslims there is no greater crime than abjuring Islam. Yezidis were thus accused of Satan worship and abnormal and immoral practices. These stories were relayed by Western travellers, ever curious for exotic tidbits, and linger even today. These stereotypes inspired countless persecutions and massacres of Yezidis, especially under Ottoman rule.

Actually, the Yezidis do not practice devil worship. Their religion is one of the surviving offshoots of Mazdeism, the set of beliefs that was the basis for the reforms of Zoroaster (better known as Nietzsche's Zarathustra), who lived between 1400 and 1200 BCE. The Yezidis are thought to be a branch of the *Majous* called *zerdachis* (Zoroastrians) in Iran, and recognized as a "People of the Book" by Caliph Omar, who succeeded Mohammad. Indeed, Mazdeism can be considered one of the precursors of monotheism, and the fact that it is included in the Qur'an should enable Yezidis to enjoy protection in any Muslim country.

The word Yezidi could be derived from a Persian word, *yezd*, signifying God. The letters YZD, in cuneiform writing, have been found on clay tablets from ancient times, attesting to an extremely early presence in Mesopotamia.

According to the Yezidis, God forgave Satan his refusal to kneel before Adam, and reintegrated him among the angels 7,000 years later. The Devil as the Angel of Evil thus does not exist. They call him Taus Malek, the Peacock Angel, and never use the names given by the Christians and Muslims. The words "Devil," "Satan," or "*Iblis*" (or *Shitan* in Arabic) are, for Yezidis, grave insults.

The Yezidis believe in metempsychosis, the transmigration of souls. They do not proselytize, for they claim to be of a different breed from the rest of humanity. According to one of their legends, they are the direct descendants of Adam, born from a jar filled with a mix of Adam's seed and clay.

Yezidis pray morning and evening facing the sun, and they bury their dead so that they face the mausoleum of Shaykh Adi, their principal saint. He is interred in the Lalish Valley in the *Shaykhan* (the "country of shaykhs"), a portion of Kurdistan situated about twenty miles (30 km) north of Mosul. Mainly farmers, and tobacco growers, Yezidis are primarily found throughout Kurdistan, and in the Sinjar Mountains in Iraq and Syria, where they form the majority. Their principal holy sites are also found in this region.

Some Yezidis live in the Caucasus, in Armenia and in Germany, among the Turkish immigrant community. They are led by an emir (prince) who is a descendant of Shaykh Adi, and lives in Iraq. Their community is divided into tribes and castes.

Sinjar

Sinjar is located 75 miles (120 km) east of Mosul at the foot of the southern face of Sinjar Jebel, which tops out at about 4,500 feet. It is on the site of the ancient city of Singara. In the third century, Sinjar was a fortified Roman town, built to contain a Parthian advance. Traces of ramparts built at the time are still visible.

The minaret of Sinjar, with its cylindrical trunk, is a vestige of a mosque built by the *attabegs* of Mosul in 1169, and one of the oldest minarets in Iraq. About 35 feet high, it is decorated with Thuluth calligraphy. This was a style codified by vizier Ibn Mukla in the 9th century to replace the famous Kufic, which was judged to be too rigid and illegible.

Sitta Zinab, the martyr Hussein's sister, is said to have passed by here, en route to Syria, where she is buried. A hilltop sanctuary is dedicated to her. One can see its distinctive green walls from afar.

The other interesting religious edifices of the region are: the monument of Zachariah (a Biblical Prophet), an old church dedicated to Saint George (the patron saint of the city's Christians), and the mausoleums of Hassan and Hussein (the sons of Ali). At the entrance of the city, coming from Mosul, one passes by three Yezidi tombs; they are one of the most important religious communities of the region.

The Jebel is not easy to access. It was long used as a refuge by religious and political dissidents. Behind Sinjar, a recently built road snakes up the mountain in a series of hairpin turns. It leads to a valley populated by Yezidi families. Tobacco grown in the region is sold in the markets at Mosul.

Ba'shiqa

Ba'shiqa ("the abode of the oppressor," in Aramaic) is situated in the foothills of Kurdistan, 12 miles (20 km) northeast of Mosul. It has existed since before Christian times.

Tell Billa, a nearby mound, was excavated by Victor Place and Sir Henry Layard, who discovered raw bricks and pottery. In 1933, the site was identified as that of the Assyrian city of Sibanipa.

Today, the majority of the inhabitants of Ba'shiqa are Yezidis. Their cone-topped temples dot the surrounding hillsides. They live in harmony with Muslims and Christians (who are mostly Jacobites). The latter speak Arabic rather than Syriac, and are originally from Tikrit.

In the 13th century, waterwheels irrigated the gardens and the olive, date, and citrus groves. The city's oil, soap, and *arak* are still highly reputed.

Near the ruins of al-Qalaa, an ancient citadel, the caves of the Valley of Monks, with their cisterns carved in the rock, are all that remains of a monastery.

Bahzani

A mile and a half from Ba'shiqa, the picturesque village of Bahzani (which means "Revolution" in Aramaic) is also peopled by Yezidis and Jacobites, who are rumored in the region to possess gifts of clairvoyance. Caves located near a spring are called al-Banat, or Convent of the Virgins.

Fire ceremony in a Yezidi sanctuary at Ba'shiqa

── SIXTEEN ──

From Baghdad to Khanaqin

This route through the Diyala River Valley is known as the road of kings.

Ba'quba

Ba'quba is a very old city. Its name is Aramaic, meaning the "House of Jacob" (*Ba'Yaquba*). Its strategic position on the road to Iran, 41 miles (66 km) northeast of Baghdad, as well as its fertile land, has made it a prosperous city since ancient times. Its vegetable gardens have supplied Baghdad's needs since the Abbasid Caliphate.

Khanaqin

A small city situated on the frontier with Iran, on the road of Persian invasions, of Shi'ite pilgrimages for Karbala and Najaf, and of caliphs going to Khorassan. Intense fighting took place in this region during the Iran–Iraq War.

Khanaqin's period of glory was during the Sassanids' reign. A bridge of brick and plaster that crosses the Hulwan dates from that time.

The region is famed for its tasty fruits and vegetables, notably pomegranates, lemons, and figs.

The Ahl-i-Haqq, "Sons of Benjamin"

In the high country of Qasr al-Chirin, a small city located on the Iranian side of the border, one can visit the tomb of the Prophet Benjamin (Pir-Benyamin). He is venerated by the *Ahl-i-Haqq*, the "Faithful of the Truth."

In Iraq, they are often called *qaqai*, or brothers. They are Kurds from the region of Khanaqin, or Kurds living in Kirkuk or Mosul.

The community of "Faithful of the Truth" was founded in the 14th–15th centuries by Sultan Sohak, the fourth and last incarnation of God. The sect counts approximately 800,000 members, in Iraq, Iran, Turkey, India, and Afghanistan. Some Jewish scholars think that the "Faithful" are Muslims of the Benjaminite tradition, descendants of the Jewish tribe of Benjamin. Others say that the sect is closer to the Septimal Shi'ites beliefs and traditions.

Little is known about this esoteric sect; its sacred writings are kept secret. The *qaqai* often hide their religious affiliation, to avoid the risk of being ostracized as heretics. Their doctrine is apparently close to Shi'ism, but also contains numerous reminiscences of Mazdeism and Manicheism. They believe in the transmigration of souls, and in reincarnation. In their dogma, Ali, the Fourth Caliph, is one of God's incarnations.

The *Ahl-i-Haqq* consider Benjamin (to whom God later gave the name Gabriel) to be the first of angels. For them, he is a spiritual Adam.

SEVENTEEN

From Baghdad to Haditha

This journey traverses the Upper Euphrates Valley, as the famous Caliph Harun al-Rashid once did to reach his summer home in Ana, the last major city before the Syrian border.

Al-Ambar

An ancient city in lush farm country on the east bank of the Euphrates, 38 miles (60 km) from Baghdad, al-Ambar is home to Tell Aswad, whose ruins date from 3000 BCE. In the third century, it was called Firoz Shapur (Shapur the Victorious) after the Persian conqueror Shapur I (241–272) who had built a citadel there to keep watch over the irrigation canals.

In the sixth century, Firoz Shapur became al-Ambar, which means simply "depot," in reference to the extensive storehouses that were part of the citadel.

In addition to the majority Muslims, al-Ambar's population included numerous religious minorities, such as Nestorians, Jacobites, and Jews. The famous idol, Hubal, which Mohammad destroyed, came from al-Ambar.

Al-Ambar was seized in 634 by the Muslim troops of Khalid; Iraq's third mosque was built there subsequently. In the 8th century, Caliph al-Mansur made the city his capital while awaiting the completion of Baghdad.

In 1262, the city was destroyed by the Mongols, and part of its population slaughtered.

Habbaniyya Lake

A canal brings floodwaters of the Euphrates to this lake near Ramadi, allowing it to play an important regulatory role in the river system. A well-appointed tourist complex is here, 52 miles (84 km) west of Baghdad, with a four-star hotel, several pools and villas, and sailing.

There is also an air base at Habbaniyya, built by the British. It was besieged by the Iraqi Army during Rashid Ali's 1941 Revolution. The Arab Legion was sent to break the siege, and retake Baghdad.

Ramadi

Built by the Turkish Governor Midhat Pasha (1869–1872), Ramadi boasts suburbs latticed by a dense network of canals irrigating rich farmland. Sixty-five miles (105 km) west of Baghdad, Ramadi is visible from the overpass of the Baghdad-Amman highway, which passes close by, with a good view of the Euphrates as well.

Hit

Hit is built on two hills that dominate the west bank of the Euphrates 115 miles (185 km) west of Baghdad. These hills could be artificial: perhaps they contain the ruins of a city already existing in the 9th century BCE. It was then known as Id, from the Assyrian word for tar, *iddu* or *ittu*, which was its main export. In antiquity, tar had important uses: it was an ingredient in the mortar used in the building of cities such as Babylon, and it was a sealant for the boats that plied Iraq's inland navigation system. These boats were made of mulberry and tamarind branches, lashed with reed and straw, and sealed with a layer of tar. And, Hit is said to have been saved from epidemics by the presence of sulfur and tar vapors in the air.

A few miles from Hit, one can visit the ruins of a mysterious city called Ulayya al-Ma'qluba, the "Changeling City."

In the Middle Ages, cereal and date plantations whose fruits were sung by the poet Abu Nawas contributed to the prosperity of Hit and its region.

Haditha

Haditha was founded by Caliph Omar, on an island in the Euphrates where there had been a fortress, 162 miles (260 km) from Baghdad.

There are still beautiful *norias* or waterwheels that supply river water along a vast network of irrigation canals. The city is renowned for its fruit orchards and date-palm plantations.

North of Haditha, on the west bank of the Euphrates, near ancient limestone quarries, several mausoleums are visible, one of which is devoted to passengers of Noah's Ark.

A Baghdad–Haditha railroad link, inaugurated in the 1990s, was supposed to be the first stage in a line that would connect the Persian Gulf to the Mediterranean.

Ana

The last sizeable Iraqi city before the Syrian border at Raqqa, 205 miles (330 km) from Baghdad, Ana was the summer residence of none other than Harun al-Rashid. The ancient city, known at the time as Anatho, extended over six miles along the west bank of the Euphrates. Today, it is covered over by a reservoir, and a new city has been built on higher ground.

For centuries, a bitter feud opposed the cities of Ana and neighboring Rawa, on the opposite side of the river. A "peace" was signed in 1921, but the rivalry lingers to this day.

Some of Iraq's most beautiful norias (waterwheels) are in Haditha

— EIGHTEEN —

From Baghdad to Erbil (via Kirkuk)

The road is good, if a bit monotonous. Exiting Baghdad, follow the signs for Kirkuk, via Hib Hib and Khalis, or take the road that goes through Ba'quba, if you want to visit the plain of the Diyala River, with its vegetable and date-palm plantations. From there, head toward the Khan Seyyid palm oasis for 42 miles (67 km), then toward Delli Abbas, through an area planted with fruit trees. One can see in the distance the highlands of the Jebel Hamrin, and soon the road begins to snake through hilly country. The road crosses the Nahrin Su (270 feet above sea level) and its fertile valley, arriving at Salahiyeh (Kufri in Kurdish, 117 miles (187 km) from Baghdad), then at Aq Su (the "White Water", or *Nahr Abyad* in Arabic, *Av-I-Spi* in Kurdish). These wadis swell suddenly during periods of heavy rain. Just before Tuz Khurmati ("Salt and Dates"), the road traverses a mountainous defile between Neft Dagh and Ali Dagh. The road ascends brusquely. At Dohuk (162 miles / 260 km), one finds the sanctuary of Zain al-Abidin, recognizable by its four white domes. From there Kirkuk is reached after crossing a stretch of rocky country.

After Kirkuk, heading toward Erbil, the air becomes charged with sulfur vapors. At certain places, gas coming up from the ground can be lit up with a match. Near Baba Gurgur, there is a source of sulfur-rich water. Before reaching Altun Kopru (218 mi / 340 km), where the road crosses the Lesser Zab, one can see, in the distance toward the west, Jebel Makhoul, rising on the other side of the Tigris. A few miles further, the citadel of Erbil appears on the horizon.

Kirkuk and the Eternal Flame

Kirkuk, 168 miles (270 km) north of Baghdad, is the seat of the governorate (*muhafaza*) of al-Ta'mim. "Al-Ta'min means "state-owned," a nod to the Iraqi government's nationalization of foreign oil assets in 1972.

In antiquity, the region was called Beth Garmai "the Country of Bones." The *qala'a* (citadel) is perched on an artificial hill that rises above the city and is said to contain the vestiges of the ancient Sumerian city of Arapha. Arapha is now the name of one of the city's neighborhoods, a residential area generally populated by Iraqi Petroleum Company (IPC) engineers.

Kirkuk was first called Karkha, then Karkh Yasdin, in homage to an illustrious native, who had been the court silversmith for Chosroes II. Later, the city became an important Nestorian religious center, and grew further under Ottoman rule.

A few miles away, near Baba Gurgur, the first oil well drilled by the IPC, the flames of the Eternal Fire burn out of the ground. Nearby a temple to the goddess Anahita once stood, as well as a furnace mentioned by the Prophet Daniel in the Old Testament. During World War I, the British attempted without success to bomb the site, in order to put out the fire that lit the sky for enemy warplanes.

The city and its environs have a strong minority population of Kurds and Turkomans. The latter are descendants of mercenaries that fought for the Abbasids, or of the Black or White Sheep horde that successively invaded Iraq in the 15th century. Most of them are Sunni, except for a few pockets of Shi'a Turkomans in certain villages, belonging to the *kizilbash* sect ("Red Heads" in Turkish).

Kirkuk, World Oil Capital

The history of petroleum as we know it only begins in 1859, with its first industrial exploitation in the United States. The rumble that announced a geyser of oil near Baba Gurgur in October 1927 intrigued the local bedouins, but it did not impress them. In Iraq, petroleum had been known since ancient times.

Noah's Ark was sealed with bitumen, as were the drains found in Iraq dating from the time of al-Obeid (4000 BCE). Herodotus and Strabo describe its use by the Babylonians in the construction of buildings and even roads. Pliny, the Roman historian, noted that petroleum was used instead of oil in lamps, and that people burned tar to drive away insects from cultivated fields.

Naphtha was used in Hatra, near Mosul, to manufacture incendiary devices, long before the invention of the "Greek fires." According to the Roman historian Ammianus Marcellinus, the Medes of Persia tipped their reed arrows with a receptacle containing flammable material. In the 8th century, Arabs started to trade in the first incendiary grenades. In the 13th century, the use of petroleum weaponry was so generalized that oil was being extracted throughout Mesopotamia and Persia, and exported in quantity to Egypt and India. The refining process has been known since the first centuries of Christian times. The more complex process of "cracking," though only codified in the United States in 1861, was being practiced in the 11th century by Arabs in the Damascus region.

The first scientific studies of petroleum deposits in Iraq were conducted in the latter part of the 19th century by French and German geologists (Jacques de Morgan, 1882; Baron von Oppenheim, 1899).

The first war for oil began around the project for a Berlin–Baghdad railroad line. An Armenian by the name of Calouste Gulbenkian succeeded in interesting Sultan Abdul Hamid in oil prospecting, so much so that the Sultan decreed that all future oil revenues would belong to him. Since the visit of Kaiser Wilhelm II to Constantinople in 1898, the Germans' influence had grown with the Ottoman Empire, and they had obtained control over the Anatolian railroad in 1903. They also had prospecting and extraction rights on all oil deposits that would be discovered on a band of territory 12 miles (20 km) wide, centered along the railroad.

This state of affairs was not to the liking of the British, who had long understood the strategic value of petroleum, and had no desire to see the Germans planted in Mesopotamia, along a vitally important route to India. The Foreign Office maneuvered cleverly. After the deposition of Sultan Abdul Hamid in 1909, the British founded the Turkish Petroleum Company (TPC) and integrated the Deutsche Bank, which as a result ended up not having sufficient funds to finance the railroad.

For many historians, Iraqi oil is intimately linked to the aftermath of

The Tomb of Daniel (Nabi Daniyal)

The Prophet Daniel (a name signifying "God judges me") was the chief astrologer of Nabuchadnezzar II. This king believed Daniel's gifts of divination and interpretation to be ten times better than all the magicians and astrologers of Mesopotamia. Daniel is said to have lived until the time of Cyrus the Great, who was the last of the Neo-Babylonian kings.

The Old Testament recounts that Nabuchadnezzar II had had a huge golden statue of Daniel built, and ordered his people to worship him. Later, under Nabonides, Daniel had a vision of four monstrous heads rearing up over his statue, and dying one by one at its feet. He interpreted this to signify the imminent demise of the four great ancient empires: Babylonian, Medo-Persian, Greek, and Roman.

For certain Iraqis who come to visit the sanctuary, Daniel's vision is a very present one. They see the influence of the four great powers of World War II as being on the decline. Great Britain and France have lost their colonial empires. The Soviet Union has collapsed. The United States is the fourth, the "different beast," the one that the prophecy says wants to "change the times and the laws."

Daniel is also known for having foreseen the fall of Babylon. One day, during a banquet organized by the court of Balthazar (prince of Babylon and son of Nabonides), a series of incomprehensible words appeared on the whitewashed walls of the palace: "Mene, Tekel, Parsin." The Queen, terrified, summoned Daniel, who immediately understood: "God has counted your reign," he said. "He has ended it. Your kingdom will be divided among the Medes and the Persians." That night, Balthazar was assassinated, and the Persian Cyrus took over Babylon.

For Muslims, the words deciphered by Daniel were written in Arabic. They were preceded by the formula "In the name of Allah the Merciful."

According to the Arab historian al-Thalabi, Daniel's body was found in a trunk sealed with lead during the taking of Susa by the Muslims. The mysterious corpse, covered in a golden shroud, was identified by Ali during a meeting of the Companions of the Prophet, called for the purpose by Caliph Omar.

Daniel's body was thrown in the river, to prevent its becoming an object of adoration. Later, the coffin was unearthed and exposed on the banks of the Tigris, so that the local inhabitants could benefit from its supposed virtuous powers. Then, it was hung underneath a bridge, in the middle of the river. Finally, to end the superstitious behavior, Daniel's remains were interred near Kirkuk.

In the region of Kirkuk, one can also visit the tombs of Sadrach and Meshack, whom the Old Testament says were thrown into a burning furnace by Nabuchadnezzar, only to come out alive. The tomb of their companion, Abed Nego, has disappeared.

World War I. From the beginning of the conflict, German assets in the TPC were frozen. After the war, France, which had been late in realizing the importance of oil, traded the *vilayat* of Mosul against participation in the Iraqi Petroleum Company (the IPC had replaced the TPC). After the overthrow of the monarchy in Iraq on July 14, 1958, and until the IPC's nationalization on June 1, 1972, oil was a source of numerous conflicts between Baghdad and London. And given London's support of the 2003 war in Iraq, some might argue that it is still a source of conflict between the two countries. It is just that the United States has largely taken over Britain's earlier interest in the region.

Altun Kopru

Altun Kopru, "Golden Bridge" in Turkmen, was known in antiquity as Simirrun. This fortified village was situated, originally, on an island in the Lesser Zab. The "Path of the King" that linked Anatolia to Seleucia, via Zakho, made its bridges a strategic passage. Tamerlane took this road on his way to destroy Baghdad.

The village grew in importance in the 12th century with the construction of two stone bridges meant to improve traffic along the caravan line from Mosul to Baghdad. Merchants found the tolls levied exorbitant, so they named them the "Golden Bridges." The city, called Qantara al-Zab ("bridge over the Zab"), is peopled by Arabs, Turkomans, and Kurds. The ancient bridges were destroyed by the Turkish army in 1918, retreating before the British advance.

Yorghan Tepe

Digs have revealed that the site of Yorghan Tepe (*tepe* means "tell" in Persian), 9 miles (15 km) southwest of Kirkuk, was occupied since the fourth millennium BCE. Archaeologists have discovered the remains of the Sumerian town of Ga-Sur (third millennium BCE), as well as those of Nuzi, an important town dating from the time of the Mittanian Empire, which extended from Syria to the Zagros Mountains during the 15th and 14th centuries BCE.

A palace and several temples have been unearthed, including walls decorated with frescoes and sculpted pilasters.

Jarmo and Barda Balka

Discovered in 1948 near Shemshemal, Jarno is one of the oldest known Neolithic villages in the world. It lies just 37 miles (59 km) from Kirkuk, in the direction of Sulaimaniya. Sixteen distinct layers of habitation have been exposed, spanning a period of 500 years from about 6500 to 6000 BCE. Animal statuettes and feminine figurines have been found there.

Nearby, Barda Balka (in Kurdish, the "raised stone") and its megalith are the site of discoveries of elephant and rhinoceros bones, as well as some rudimentary utensils, dating from about 80,000 years ago.

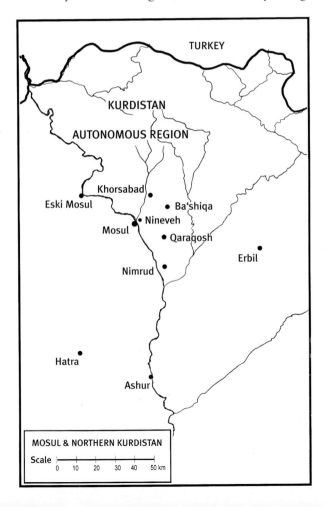

— NINETEEN —

The Kurdistan Autonomous Region

As was true throughout the country, the situation in Iraqi Kurdistan got worse after the first Gulf War. Although economic conditions remained better under the US-imposed sanctions in the Kurdish north than in center and southern Iraq, life was still very difficult. Until the 2003 war, it was not even possible to visit the region coming from Baghdad. Before that time two rival chiefs, Massud Barzani and Jalal Talabani, each governed a portion of territory, and their partisans periodically fought over questions of land and taxation rights on oil tankers that travel between Turkey and Iraq, transiting through Kurdistan. Barzani is the son of the legendary independence leader Mustafa Barzani and controlled Erbil and the region north of Mosul to the Turkish border. Jalabani controlled the region along the Iranian border, centered around Sulaimaniya, his hometown.

The divisions between the Kurds, which stem from ancestral enmities between clans and the personal ambitions of their leaders, have always rendered the people vulnerable and confused, easy prey for foreign powers' intervention. The Ottomans, then modern Turkey, the Germans, the British, the Soviets, then the Russians, the Americans, the Israelis, the Iranians, and the Syrians have all faced off against each other through rival Kurdish chiefs.

Upon taking power in 1968, the Ba'ath party had as its primary objective consolidating its power and establishing peaceful relations among the country's many peoples, including the Kurds. Any Iraqi government must face resolving the Kurdish question, at once maintaining Iraq's own national integrity, while recognizing some version of Kurdish aspirations. At different times, these aspirations have included calls for independence, for autonomy within a unified Iraq, cultural autonomy, and other forms of Kurdish identity.

On March 11, 1970, a proclamation laying a promising starting-point for future Iraqi-Kurdish relations (see sidebar) was made public, followed four years to the day later by a law granting internal autonomy to regions with a Kurdish majority. The governorates of Sulai-maniyya, Erbil, and Dohuk created the Kurdistan Autonomous Region.

At this time, Mustafa Barzani, who had negotiated the project with then Vice President Saddam Hussein, and who was initially favorable to the Ba'athists' proposal, abruptly did an about-face. He had been promised support and encouraged by the United States, the Shah of Iran, and Israel to rise up against Baghdad. But with the signing of the Algiers Accord between Iran and Iraq, all of these supporters soon abandoned the Kurds, contributing in no small way to the demise of Kurdish guerrillas' hopes for success a few years later. Henry Kissinger, then Secretary of State, is reported to have said, "covert action is not to be confused with missionary work."

Throughout the Iran–Iraq war, armed Kurdish opposition movements, led by Massoud Barzani and Jalal Talabani, allied themselves with Iran. Iraq's government responded by unleashing Operation Anfal. A 19-mile (30-km) security band was created along the border with Iran. Numerous villages were destroyed and their inhabitants killed or deported; thousands of Kurds were victims. Later,

View of Aqra, in Kurdistan

after the 1991 Gulf War, the Kurds reproached the US for not having kept their promises. The creation of an exclusive zone in the north of Iraq, watched over by American and British planes, finally allowed them to take administrative control for themselves for 12 years, though not without bloody internal conflicts and tension with Baghdad.

The histories of Kurdish political leaders show, in sharp focus, the effects on a people caught between nations more powerful than their own, desperately scrambling for their own identity.

Take Jalal Talabani. He has been nicknamed the "king of mercenaries" by former allies who he has rejected (yet who still expect favors). A couple decades ago, he declared himself anti-imperialist, anti-Zionist, and even Maoist. He was once close to George Habash, a leader of the Popular Front for the Liberation of Palestine (PFLP). Now, Talabani is a touted ally of the US occupation. Yet many Kurds remember that he rallied to Baghdad's side against Kurdish rival Mustafa Barzani.

Massud Barzani, who inherited the leadership of the Kurdistan ratic Party (KDP) from his father, has long reason to suspect international promises of help to the Kurds. At age 30, he witnessed the abandonment of the Kurdish guerillas led by his father after the signing of the Algiers Accord in March 1975. He settled down in Iran to restructure his troops. In 1991, he saw the US government allow Saddam Hussein to brutally crush the rebellion the US itself had encouraged. This lead to the deaths of thousands and the displacement of many more Kurds, who fled to the Turkish and Iranian borders.

In August 1996, he appealed to Saddam Hussein to reestablish order at Erbil, and put a stop to the actions of Talabani, supported by Washington, and those of Iran, with an eye on the whole of northern Iraq. Were it not for intense American pressure against him, Barzani might have reached an agreement with Baghdad.

It is yet to be seen how the 2003 war and occupation will play out for the Kurds.

Erbil

Erbil (or *Hawler* in Kurdish), 211 miles (340 km) north of Baghdad, is the capital of the Kurdistan Autonomous Region. It is also one of the oldest continuously inhabited cities in the world, since the second millenium BCE, lying as it does on the strategic caravan route to India and China. Erbil is known to historians for a famous battle that took

The citadel of Erbil

place in the plain between Mosul and Erbil, during which Alexander the Great crushed the Persian Darius III in 331 BCE.

The ancient tell has not yet been explored. The stone wall of the citadel dominates the plain of Adiaben, some fifty yards below. It contains three separate quarters: al-Sarray, al-Takia, and al-Tokhana, and a total of 500 houses. Long ago, people got to the fort by two narrow streets, one reserved for men, and one for women. Today, one of these streets has been enlarged to allow vehicle access.

Several houses were restored before the Gulf War, and turned into hotels, exhibit areas, or restaurants. Some still have intact decorations and ornate ceilings. A house attributed to Mulla Saleh has been transformed into a museum and library. An 18th-century *hammam* (bath house) has also been restored.

Erbil was one of Assyria's great religious cities, second only to Ashur. It was referred to as Arba Ellu (the Four Gods) and Ishtar reigned supreme in the divine pantheon. Romans called it Arbira. After having defeated the Sassanids at Ctesiphon in 216, Emperor Caracalla took the citadel and, in a gesture of revenge against the Parthians, had their kings' tombs desecrated. Erbil was converted to Christianity early on, and remained the seat of a bishopric until the ninth century.

In 1167, the Kurdish Emir Zain al-Din Begtegin founded a principality with Erbil as its capital. He controlled a region that extended from Sinjar to Harran and Tikrit. In the lower part of the city, the octagonal foundation of a 12th-century minaret is all that remains of the *madrasa* (school) al-Muzzafariyya, built by Muzzafar al-Kokburi, one of his descendants.

Erbil was attacked by the Mongols in 1235, but the Kurds retained control of the citadel until 1258, when the Mongols, with the complicity of Badr Eddin Lulu, finally took it. A Christian governor was appointed (perhaps because Hulagu's mother was a Nestorian), but he was soon revoked and put to death by torture. After the Mongols massacred many of Erbil's inhabitants, in 1309 the Christians emigrated to Mosul.

Since 1968, Erbil has been home to various industries, including tobacco processing, rugs, and dairy products; but with the international embargo of the 1990s, these activities were sharply curtailed.

From Erbil to the Iranian Border

Exiting Erbil, take Hamilton's Road, named after the engineer from New Zealand who built it in the 1930s. The road itself, as it existed in antiquity, linked Azerbaijan (then northwestern Iran) to the Mediterranean. Today, the road passes the villages of Salaheddin (1,090m/3,576ft), and Shaqlawa (565m/1,800ft), perched on the flanks of the Safin Mountains; both were prized summer retreats for Iraqis before the Gulf War. The road then rises. Atop a spur of the Hanir Dagh, lie the ruins of the castle of Princess Zad. Soon, one crosses the Spilik Pass. About 12 miles (20 km) on, before hitting the Rawandouz Gorge, look for the admirable Gali Ali Beg waterfall.

The Gali Ali Beg gorge, named after a legendary Yezidi shaykh, became the first caravan path through this long impenetrable area. The road continues through the mountains, higher and higher. At Kani Rash, Hamilton discovered the ruins of a bridge built by Harun al-Rashid. Near the Gorges of Berserini, there are numerous caves, such as the Kospsypsy Cave.

After Rayat, one reaches Hajj Omran (1780m/5840ft), where, theoretically at least—if there is snow, and not too much political conflict—one can ski. Iran lies just beyond.

Rawandouz

The strategic importance of this city is obvious when one comes upon it, perched on a rocky escarpment at about 3,000 feet. It controls the road leading to Iran, and the network of mule paths that crisscross Kurdistan. The river of Rawandouz and its tributaries have dug out impressive canyons on their way to the Greater Zab, which in turn traverses the spectacular Bekhme Gorge. Indeed, the beauty of this region is so renowned that Nestorians situate the legendary Garden of Eden here. A few Christian villages subsisted until World War I, but relations with the Kurds soured when they helped Russians bomb the city in 1915.

The history of Rawandouz is indeed a sad sequence of strife. Most of the city's rulers have met violent deaths. Among the best known, in the early 19th century, was Mohammad Khor, "the Blind," who rose up against the Turks, and imposed his authority all the way to Erbil and

Sakho. Defeated, he was imprisoned in Constantinople, then pardoned—but only to be assassinated on his way home.

The Cave of Shanidar

Situated in the Jebel Baradost, about 12 miles (20 km) from Rawanouz, in the Greater Zab Valley, this cave boasts traces of human habitation from 50,000 years ago. These traces include human remains, a skeleton resting on a bed of branches, and evidence of animal domestication, notably sheep.

In the Jebel Baradost, near Havdian, the treasure of an Assyrian king is supposed to be hidden. According to local tradition, it bedecked the temples of a city whose ruins are located nearby, called the "city of the cruel people."

From Erbil to Mosul

The road runs along the mountains of Kurdistan, and crosses the Greater Zab, a tributary of the Tigris, reaching Qaramless, a village near the site of the Battle of Erbil (331 BCE). Rejoin Aqra after crossing a tributary of the Zab, 25 miles (40 km) from Mosul. About 12 miles further north, the caves of Gunduk boast beautiful Assyrian reliefs of hunting scenes.

Barzan

A Kurdish village situated on the east bank of the Greater Zab, 50 miles (80 km) north of Erbil, Barzan is the center of the Barzani tribe, whose shaykhs have always had a reputation for being troublemakers. In Ottoman times, they were quasi-autonomous, until the Turks took prisoner Shaykh Abdel Salim Iraq in 1915, and hanged him. His successor, Shaykh Ahmad, is thought to have temporarily converted to Christianity. His brother is the famous Mustafa Barzani, the father of Massoud, currently the head of one of the two main Kurdish political parties, the Kurdish Democratic Party (see the opening of this chapter).

Qaramless

Qaramless is first documented in Assyrian tablets under the name of Qarmess, which means "destroyed village." The two neighboring tells have not yet given up their secrets. In 1840, the British archaeologist Layard unearthed Assyrian bricks in one of them, and Victor Place, his French colleague, a set of stone walls that apparently date from Sassanid times.

The Battle of Erbil (Arbales) took place nearby, in the plain of Gaugameles. One of the generals, Darius or Alexander (historians are not sure which) watched the fight from the top of Tell al-Ganem, near the entrance of the village that faces Mosul.

Sulaimaniya

Sulaimaniya was built in 1784 in a hollow high up in the mountains, at 3,000 feet. It gets its name from Sulaiman Pasha, a Georgian *mameluk*, who was governor of Baghdad at the time.

During the Ottoman Empire, this part of Kurdistan was governed by chiefs of the Baban tribe, whose ancestors are said to include a young Frenchwoman taken prisoner in the 16th century. After the fall of the Baban, whom the Turks found too independent, power passed to the Barzenji tribe.

After 1919, Shaykh Mahmud Barzenji, local chief of the *qadriya*, led an uprising in the region against the British. After refusing to participate in the election of Faisal I to the throne of Iraq, he was deported to India. But unrest in the region became only worse, so the British had to

Sulaimaniya in 1950

authorize Barzenji's return to Kurdistan, where he promptly proclaimed himself *hukmdar* (king) in October 1922. Furious, the British bombed the city several times, killing nearly all its inhabitants (the population fell from 20,000 to about 700).

Today, Sulaimaniya is the center of the governorate that bears its name. Tobacco and leather processing industries prosper, or used to, alongside most of the Kurdish-language publishing houses.

The region also is home to several prehistoric sites. In the Darbendkawa, a narrow pass northwest of the city, one can admire reliefs depicting the victory of the Akkadian king, Naram Sin (2291–2255 BCE). Not far from there, Mt. Nisir is the place where Utnapishtim's ark came to rest in the Gilgamesh epic.

Summer resorts at Sarnashar, a few miles from Sulaimaniya, or at Ahmad Awa, almost 50 miles away (75 km), attracted droves of Iraqis until the Gulf War. The lake near the Dokan dam, where one can go boating and even pedal-boating, also has a 5-star hotel. Lake Derbandikan, 40 miles (65 km) away, is reserved for sailing.

The Caves of Zarzi

At Zarzi, near Qala Dizeh, in the valley of the Lesser Zab, two prehistoric caves date human occupation of the area to 12,000 years ago. Tombs dug 25 feet deep in the limestone reveal a funeral chamber, an altar, a fireplace, and trays for offerings.

Dohuk and Environs

The roads in this area snake along sheer mountain walls and through narrow gorges. Luckily, they are relatively well maintained. The rugged but charming landscape is a paradise for hunters: wild boars, wild goats, and hares abound, as well as porcupines, a favorite of the local Christian mountain people. In summertime, people from Mosul flock to the cool air of Zawitha (1422m/4665ft) and its fir trees, Zawaretuka (1675m/5495ft) nestled in cypress and maple groves, or Sarsang (1046m/4243ft) and its nearby springs.

Dohuk itself, 45 miles (73 km) from Mosul, is the seat of one of the Autonomous Regions' two governorates. Known as Dastagard under the Persian occupation, it is situated at 2,000 feet. In front of the village, a tell contains the vestiges of an Assyrian fortress.

Nemrik

A village thought to be nearly 10,000 years old was discovered in 1987 at Nemerik, north of Dohuk. The houses were built about 5 feet above ground level, of earth bricks, with no windows. One entered through the roof by way of a ladder. The streets of this village were paved with stones gathered from the banks of the Tigris.

Amadiyya

This northernmost town of Iraq, 62 miles (100 km) north of Mosul, gets its name from Imad Eddin Zangi, who rebuilt the fortress in 1142. There are huge cisterns dug into the rock to capture rainfall for drinking water. Amadiyya occupies a strategic position, dominating the valleys of the Greater Zab and the Khabur.

Zawita

The environs of Zawita, 11 miles (17 km) from Dohuk, are covered with a pine forest said to date from Assyrian times. There is a popular tourist hostel operating in the summer, when political conditions allow.

Souara Touga

A tourist resort situated 14 miles (22 km) from Zawita, at 4,600 feet, Souara Touga is surrounded by poplars and cypress, and never gets hotter than 90 degrees. The view of the valley is stunning.

Sarsang

Just before Sarsang, stop at Ashawa, a small village reputed for its waterfalls and tradition of crafts.

Zakho

Near the Turkish border, 78 miles (125 km) from Baghdad, Zakho is known for its Abbasid stone bridge over the Khabour River. It had replaced an older bridge over which the vitally important Road of Kings passed.

Fourteen miles (22 km) from Zakho, the Sharamish Falls (1350m/4429 ft) are some of the most beautiful in Kurdistan. A legend says that Noah's Ark came to rest in this region, on the Judi Dagh.

The Legend of an Abbasid Bridge

There is a story about the architect of Zakho's bridge, who couldn't get the arch to hold; each time he was ready to place the last stone, it collapsed. To explain the problem to the Emir, he told him that according to an old legend, the river would only let men dominate it after a human sacrifice. A living person must be placed inside the support, to ensure the stability of the edifice.

The Emir ordered that the first person who would be seen leaving the village heading toward the bridge be taken and entombed alive within. Alas, it was the Emir's own daughter, Dallee, who happened to be crossing the bridge. The Emir kept his word in spite of the tragic loss that would be his, and his daughter accepted the verdict without a word of protest. Only when the last stone was sealed in place, did the Emir begin to weep.

The Abbasid bridge at Zakho

Basra

GLOSSARY

attabegs: governors, under Ottoman rule

bab: gate

bema: altar which symbolizes the place where Jesus prayed

caramat: miracles

cella: the section of the sanctuary where the gods were represented

chotts: in North Africa, a vast expanse of stagnant salt water

fatwa: a ruling by Muslim authorities based on their interpretation of Islam

abaya: long tunic

hammam: bath house

imaret: people's kitchen

iwan: semi-circular vaults that open onto the courtyard and are reserved for the study of the Qur'an and hadith

keleks: rafts made of inflated bags of animal skin

khan: inns for caravans and travellers that dotted the various trade routes in the Middle East and Asia

kunasa: depot

madrasa: school

majlis: gallery

mandi: Mandean temple

maqam: ancient modes upon which Arabic music is built and contain quarter tones

masgouf: the traditional Iraqi way of cooking fish

minbar: the chair from which the imam delivers his sermon

mirhab: niche build into the wall of a mosque to indicate the direction of Mecca

moudhif: guesthouse

musala: prayer room

norias: waterwheels that supply river water to networks of irrigation canals

oud: pear-shaped fretless lute

Qa'aba: the sacred black rock that pilgrims walk around in the courtyard of the Great Mosque in Mecca

qala'a: citadel

qaqai: Kurds from the region of Khanaqin, or Kurds living in Kirkuk or Mosul

qassab: a kind of giant bamboo

rasta: Mandean traditional costume of a white cotton robe, tied at the waist with a burlap cord

serai: palace

shabbut: carp from the Tigris river

takyah: religious center

tarada: flat boats made of reeds, tightly bound and covered over in tar and petroleum

tariqa: a religious brotherhood

tell: archeology term, from the Arabic word for hill. A mound formed by the accumulated remains of ancient settlements

temenos: a rectangular esplanade surrounded by a wall of cut blocks of stone along which the merchants of the time had their boutiques

umma: community of believers in Islam; the Arab world, without boundaries

vilayat: province

zibib: a drink made from macerated raisins

ziggurat: a great tower, with steps winding around it

Kurdistan bridge

—— BIBLIOGRAPHY ——

Abd Al-Jabbar, Falih, ed. et al. *Ayatollahs, Sufis and Ideologies: State, Religion and Social Movements in Iraq*. London: Al Saqi, 2002.

Aburish, Said K. *Saddam Hussein: The Politics of Revenge*. Bloomsbury, 2000.

Alnasrawi, Abbas. *The Economy of Iraq: Oil, Wars, Destruction of Development and Prospects, 1950-2010*. Westport, CT: Greenwood Publishing Group, 1994.

Arnove, Anthony, ed. *Iraq Under Seige: The Deadly Impact of Sanctions & War*. 2nd ed. Cambridge, MA: South End Press, 2002.

Bennis, Phyllis. *Before & After: US Foreign Policy and the War on Terrorism*. Northampton, MA: Olive Branch Press, 2002.

Bennis, Phyllis, and Michel Moushabeck, eds. *Beyond the Storm: A Gulf Crisis Reader*. Northampton, MA: Olive Branch Press, 1991.

Bennis, Phyllis. *Calling the Shots: How Washington Dominates Today's UN*. Northampton, MA: Olive Branch Press, 2000.

Bennis, Phyllis. *Understanding the U.S.-Iraq Crisis: A Primer*. Washington, DC: Institute for Policy Studies, 2003.

Braude, Joseph. *The New Iraq: Rebuilding the Country for Its People, the Middle East, and the World*. New York: Basic Books, 2003.

Chaliand, Gerard, ed. *A People Without a Country: The Kurds and Kurdistan*. Foreword David McDowall. Northampton, MA: Olive Branch Press, 1993.

Cortright, David and George A. Lopez. *The Sanctions Decade: Assessing UN Strategies in the 1990s*. Boulder, CO: Lynne Reiner Publishers, 2000.

Farouk-Sluglett, Marion and Peter Sluglett. *Iraq Since 1958: From Revolution to Dictatorship*. 2nd ed. New York: I.B. Tauris, 2001.

Friedman, Alan. *Spider's Web: The Secret History of How the White House Illegally Armed Iraq*. New York: Bantam Books, 1993.

Gunter, Michael. *The Kurdish Predicament in Iraq: A Political Analysis*. New York: Palgrave Macmillan, 1997.

Hiro, Dilip. *The Longest War: The Iran-Iraq Military Conflict*. New York: Routledge, 1991.

Izady, Mehrdad. *The Kurds: A Concise Handbook*. Crane Russak & Co., 1992.

Kelly, Michael. *Martyr's Day: Chronicle of a Small War*. New York: Random House, 1992.

Mackey, Sandra. *The Reckoning: Iraq and the Legacy of Saddam Hussein*. New York: W.W. Norton & Co., 2002.

Mahajan, Rahul. *Full Spectrum Dominance: U.S. Power in Iraq and Beyond*. New York: Seven Stories Press, 2003.

Marr, Phebe. *Modern History of Iraq*. 2nd ed. Boulder, CO: Westview Press, 2003.

Matthews, Roger. *Archaeology of Mesopotamia: Theories and Approaches*. New York: Routledge, 2003.

McDowall, David. *A Modern History of the Kurds*. New York: I.B. Tauris, 1997.

Meisalis, Susan et al. *Kurdistan: In the Shadow of History*. New York: Random House, 1997.

Munthe, Turi, ed. *The Saddam Hussein Reader: Selections from Leading Writers on Iraq*. New York: Avalon Publishing Group, 2002.

Postgate, Nicholas & J.N. *Early Mesopotamia: Society and Economy at the Dawn of History*. New York: Routledge, 1994.

Roaf, Michael. *The Cultural Atlas of Mesopotamia and the Ancient Near East*. New York: Checkmark Books, 1990.

Roux, Georges. *Ancient Iraq*. 3rd ed. New York: Viking Penguin, 1993.

Sifry, Micah L. & Christopher Cerf, eds. *The Gulf War Reader: History, Documents, Opinions*. New York: Times Books, 1991.

Sifry, Micah L. & Christopher Cerf, eds. *The Iraq War Reader: History, Documents, Opinions*. Touchstone Books, 2003.

Simons, Geoff. *Imposing Economic Sanctions: Legal Remedy or Genecidal Tool*. London: Pluto Press, 1999.

Simons, Geoff. *The Scourging of Iraq*. New York: St. Martin's Press, 1996.

Simons, Geoff. *Targeting Iraq: Sanctions and Bombing in U.S. Policy*. London: Al Saqi, 2003.

Tirman, John. *Spoils of War: The Human Costs of America's Arms Trade*. New York: The Free Press, 1997.

Tripp, Charles. *A History of Iraq*. 2nd ed. New York: Cambridge University Press, 2002.

Websites

www.afsc.org/iraq: The American Friends Service Committee is the social action branch of the Quakers. They have been organizing humanitarian assistance in Iraq, carrying out educational programs and mobilizing public opposition to economic sanctions for many years.

www.baghdadmuseum.org: The website of the Baghdad Museum.

www.casi.org.uk/index.html: The Campaign Against Sanctions on Iraq (CASI) provides information about the humanitarian situation in Iraq and its context. It aims to raise awareness of the effects of sanctions on Iraq, and campaigns on humanitarian grounds for the lifting of non-military sanctions. CASI does not support or have ties to the government of Iraq.

www.cia.gov/cia/publications/factbook/geos/iz.html: The CIA's official factbook of general information on Iraq.

www.desert-rescue.org.uk: Non-affiliated group set up to look at the effects of war on children around the world.

www.electroniciraq.net: Electronic Iraq is a news portal on the U.S.-Iraq crisis published by respected Middle East alternative news publishers.

www.epic-usa.org: The Education for Peace in Iraq Center works to educate the American people and Congress about the consequences of economic sanctions and the U.S. invasion of Iraq. They provide activists "toolkits" and organize periodic lobby days in Congress.

www.ips-dc.org/iraq: The Institute for Policy Studies works to provide analysis, talking points, op-eds, primers and other educational materials on the U.S.-Iraq crisis, including work on economic sanctions, the illegality of the US war and the need for the United Nations. The Iraq index provides a comprehensive list of articles and materials since the beginning of the Iraq crisis.

www.iraqbodycount.net: The worldwide update of reported civilian deaths in the war on Iraq.

www.iraqpress.org: Independent press agency of political, economic, cultural, and social affairs. Articles appear in English and Arabic.

www.nationalgeographic.com/iraq: *National Geographic*'s online guide to articles published about Iraq, including the reports of teams that have gone into Iraq to inspect the damage from the 2003 war to important archeological sites.

www.interlinkbooks.com: The website of Interlink Publishing features numerous titles relating to the Middle East.

Ctesiphon

— NOTES —

— NOTES —